HADRIAN'S WALL

VOLUME TWO

WALL COUNTRY WALKS

HADRIAN'S WALL

VOLUME TWO
WALL COUNTRY WALKS

---

written and illustrated by

MARK RICHARDS

Bellister Castle

CICERONE PRESS
MILNTHORPE, CUMBRIA

ACKNOWLEDGEMENTS:
I would like to record my appreciation to the many people who have welcomed me and given encouragement to my quest. Notable among their number are:

Andrew Nicholson and Phil Bradley of the East Cumbria Countryside Project; David McGlade, Hadrian's Wall Development Officer; Pauline Staff of Holmhead; Richard Sim, Editor of Haltwhistle Times; Adam Slade, Manager of Birdoswald Roman Fort; Jane Brantom, Manager of the Hadrian's Wall Partnership; David Bishop of Regional Railways; Maureen Granville, Chair of Brampton Rights-of-Way Committee; Mike Jeffrey, Hadrian's Wall Area Countryside Manger, Northumberland County Council; Gill Inglesby, Rights-of-Way Officer, Cumbria County Council and Derek Proudlock, National Park Ranger for Hadrian's Wall. A special thankyou to Rodney Busby, John and Liz McGrillis of Scotby and David Taylor and Grethe Kirkebjerg of Bellister Castle.

First published 1996

ISBN 1 85284 209 1

A catalogue record for this book
is available from the British Library

To: David and Grethe
and the
Spirit of the Centre of Britain

Advice to Readers

Readers are advised that whilst every effort is taken by the author to ensure the accuracy of this guidebook, the countryside has an inevitable dynamic, and changes will occur that may affect the contents.

The publisher would welcome notes of any such changes.

For current information - refer to page 6.

CONTENTS

INTRODUCTION

This collection of country walks is the product of an extended period of careful research. It offers quality assured walking in a range of scenic settings distinctive of the area: fulfilling circular outings that give perspective to the breadth of a so frequently enchanting country, neatly held between the Tyne valley and the shores of the Solway Firth.

All too often visitors are drawn to find the Roman Wall, and are singularly disappointed. What they find is a pale shadow of the mighty white-washed mural line the Romans built. Spanning the full isthmus, that legionary collar had shackled the lines of communications of the native Caledone tribesmen and, later, Picts and Scots; it was a tour of duty on a far flung frontier, for auxiliary soldiers, a gone to the Wall experience! Even during the three hundred years of its existence it suffered breaches. So the succeeding seventeen centuries of often torrid border life have inevitably reduced all that superbly tooled masonry to a fragmentary foundation - to be rebuilt in the imagination stone by stone.

But for the protection first effected by John Clayton of Chesters in the nineteenth century, and now English Heritage, and the National Trust, there would be nothing more than a series of shallow ditches to tell of the Wall's long passing. This narrow march has all too frequently witnessed a harsh turbulence in human affairs. Turning from century to century, from peaceful farming to the cruellest of Border Reiving feuds, from mining and industry, to the transport and tourism of today. Each phase playing significant parts in moulding a landscape as richly rewarding to the curious walker as any in Britain.

This book therefore seeks to give the walking visitor the necessary breadth of vision to see beyond the Wall, to glory at a landscape as old as the hills and yet with the vitality of a gambolling lamb in springtime. The inventive walker will find many more ways to develop the walking potential of the area than this guide can hope to portray, and I encourage you to search beyond the normally accepted bounds of Wall Country to find those precious out of the way places.

The walks are depicted on simple outline diagrams, which I have termed HIGHSPY VIEWS - pay heed to their orientation. The routes are marked by outline arrows, and where the same ground is retraced this appears as a diamond symbol.

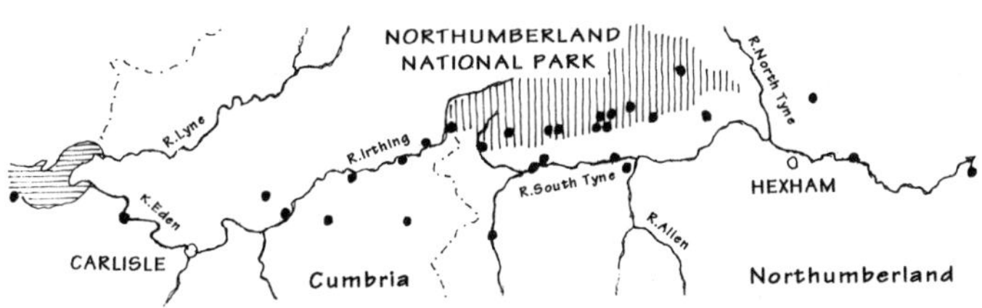

Outline map showing the location of the thirty walks featured in this guide from Prudhoe in the east to Bowness-on-Solway in the west.

Tourist Information Centres (*seasonal opening)
Brampton* 01 697 73 433
Carlisle 01 228 512 444
Corbridge* 01 434 632 815
Haltwhistle 01 434 322 002
Hexham 01 434 605 225
Longtown 01 228 791 876
Morpeth 01 670 511 323
Newcastle-upon-Tyne 01 912 620 610
Newcastle Airport 01 912 144 422
Newcastle, Central Station 01 912 300 030
Metrocentre, Gateshead 01 914 606 345
Once Brewed* 01 434 344 396
(Northumberland National Park Information Centre)
Prudhoe 01 661 833 144

English Heritage
Chesters & Corbridge 01 670 533 128
Housesteads 01 434 344 363

Other Site Museums
Birdoswald Roman Fort 01 697 747 602
Vindolanda 01 434 344 277
Carvoran Roman Army Museum
01 434 344 485

Hadrian's Wall Bus and Tyne Valley Railway
- Travel Enquiry Lines -
Cumbria County Council 01 228 812 812
Northumberland County Council 01 670 533 128

Tyne and Wear Passenger Transport Executive
01 912 325 325

ORDNANCE SURVEY MAPS
covering the area of this guide

Pathfinder - *the walker's best friend*

544 - Gretna & Eastriggs

545 - Scaleby & Brampton

546 - Haltwhistle & Gilsland

547 - Hexham & Haydon Bridge

548 - Carlisle (west) & Kirkbride

557 - Carlisle (east) & Castle Carrock

559 - Slaggyford

560 - Allendale Town & Blanchland

Landranger - *the visitor's day-trip planner*

85 - Carlisle & Solway Firth

86 - Haltwhistle, Bewcastle & Alston

87 - Hexham & Haltwhistle

88 - Tyneside & Durham

Every visitor should, as a matter of course, carry
Travelmaster 5 - Northern England

SPECIAL PLEA: Hadrian's Wall is designated a UNESCO World Heritage Site, it has been exposed to the slings and arrows of a harsh northern climate, and in the eighteen hundred years since it was abandoned, has fallen prey to all manner of wall robbing for buildings great and small. But as a tourist attraction its enduring fascination to a transitory army of visitors puts the monument, and its near environs under permanent stress. If you are visiting the area during winter months keep off the delicate turf beside the Wall. Keep the Wall 'green' by allowing the grass a chance to revive.

from LOW PRUDHOE ____________________

7¼ mile circular walk featuring:
Cherryburn, Bywell and Whittle Dene

Prudhoe Castle reflected in its moat

START grid ref. NZ 086635

As either a precursor or post-walk treat, do make a point of exploring Prudhoe Castle, a Tynedale stronghold of classic proportion and form. Knights in shining armour may no longer set forth to defend the Tyne against unwelcome guests, nonetheless, the imagination may still sally forth unshackled by time and space to when the d'Umfravilles, and later the Percys, ruled the country at large. Dating from 1173 the castle keep standing proud and free within its inner bailey, is considered to be the oldest in Northumberland. Ring: 01 661 843 276 for information.

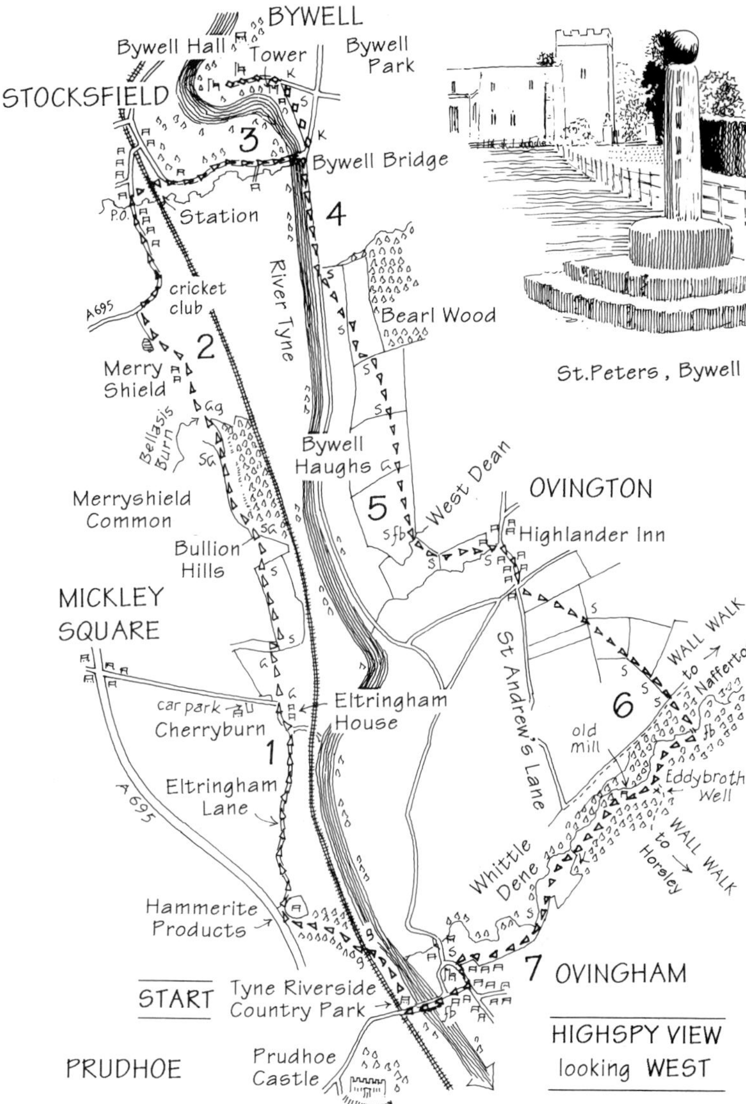

St. Peters, Bywell

Tyne Riverside Park Centre

Park at the Tyne Riverside Country Park at Low Prudhoe. Prior to embarking on the walk visit the Park Centre; information panels give a view of the work undertaken to create the linear riverbank recreational facility. Access extends downstream to Wylam via the famous Hagg Bank Bridge, structural 'test-piece' for the Tyne Bridge. Now a footbridge, Beeching axed the line in 1964. The old line was developed to Segedunum as the North Tyne Cycleway.

Ovingham across the Tyne from the Riverside Park

Leave the car park in a south-westerly direction and with all faculties alert cross the railway, via the facing hand-gates. Ascend the hollow-way through the Woodland Trust land and follow the path winding up to the Hammerite Products factory. Skirting the peripheral fence, keep below the new by-pass to enter Eltringham Lane. The rough tracked lane leads west, thankfully a peaceful passage away from the discordant hubbub of the A695. Through the bows, across the river, lies a 'ribbon' development of Lilliputian dwellings erected in the inter-war period by Geordie townsfolk wishing to secure a weekend toe-hold in the fresh country air; convenient yet sufficiently far away from the notorious urban smog. There are several strips of these 'quaint abodes' in the Ovington/Ovingham locality; the most endearing group is encountered in lower Whittle Dene towards the end of this walk. Reach the road, go left ascending to the entrance to Eltringham House Farm. Make the brief diversion 100yards further up this minor road to 'Cherryburn', the birth-place of Thomas Bewick (1753-1828). Now in the care of the National Trust,

Cherryburn

this humble cottage is open April to October (closed Tuesday and Wednesday) 1.00 p.m. - 5.30 p.m.

A remarkably perceptive artist and naturalist Bewick's wood-engravings give a unique insight into the rural life of Northumberland just before the Industrial Revolution when coal became king, and the Tyne a focus of empire. His many vignette images continue to grace books to this day. Should you be interested to learn more about the man contact: The Bewick Society (founded in 1988) via Dr. Frank Atkinson, The Old Vicarage, Ovingham, Prudhoe, Northumberland NE42 6BW   Ring 01 661 843 276.

500 yards farther up the road lies the old colliery community of Mickley Square (Mickley meaning 'big clearing'). Opposite the cross-roads visit the Thomas Bewick Gallery. For refreshment visit either the adjacent Jiggery Pokery Tea-room or the Blue Bell Inn in Mount Pleasant, which serves a very pleasant pint (author's recommendation).

Return to the farm entrance. Passing through the gate left enter the pasture, signposted 'Merry Shield'. Traverse the field to a ladder-stile/gate, bear right to another ladder-stile/gate then go left following the field boundary south-west. Cross a ladder-stile at the corner, enter the pasture bank on Bullion Hills. Bear right, sweep left in descending into the shy valley. Cross to the gate, go left along the confined pathway with steeply pitched thin bedded coal exposures in the adjacent wooded bank, continue via a stile/gate and subsequent hand-gate. Cross Bellasis Burn following an old quarry access which becomes an open track leading to Merry Shield Farm: the name means 'pleasant summer farm'. Passing the farmhouse, an agricultural contracting enterprise, follow the farm road, which is also used by waste disposal lorries accessing the old gravel pit below the farm. The track joins the A695. Go right passing the Cricket Club to enter the village of Stocksfield. Directly after crossing Stocksfield Burn, and opposite the post office/shop, bear right to enter the station. On reaching the platform go left, cross the handsome red and white cast-iron platform footbridge, proceed past the passenger shelter to exit the station. Fortunately platform tickets are not required, but perhaps you will consider becoming a passenger, using this fine facility to explore the scenic corridor through Tynedale to Carlisle, every inch the prime Wall Country of this book.

Re-gaining the road, close above Stocksfield Burn, go right to stride north to Bywell Bridge; take a moment to glance over the parapets, especially downstream.

Consider the time available, for at this point a minor spur route merits the allocation of an extra half hour to your walk. Your reward - BYWELL's tower-house and its two beautiful old churches all pleasantly set in a leafy meadow just above a sedate Tyne. Go left, diverting from the road at the kissing-gate on the left, signposted 'Bywell ¼'. Follow the fence to a stile and confined path to a second kissing-gate thus joining the road. Go left passing Bywell Castle, built from stone plundered direct from Hadrian's Wall: in tune with the fashion of the times. This

View downstream from Bywell Bridge

fifteenth century tower-house doubled as a gatehouse, a rare function of this period. The central vaulted archway is flanked by vaulted chambers, with a spiral stair leading to first floor rooms, which was lit by quite large two-light windows. The garderobe (privy) was situated in the south-west corner.

Bywell Castle

The castellated parapet was embellished with polygonal angle projections corbelled out from the rectangular corners to form open machicolations, through which defensive missiles could be cast upon hapless assailants.

Follow the peaceful road to the wayside cross which formerly lay at the hub of a vibrant community, proclaimed by Pevsner as "the most beautifully placed and the most picturesque and architecturally rewarding of all Tynedale villages". In the sixteenth century it was said that the thriving village was "inhabyted with handy craftsmen whose trade is all in yron worke". Even in the nineteenth century twenty houses were inhabited; now this parkland scene and quiet passage of the Tyne is treasured by the occupants of Bywell Hall in splendid insularity. At hand to the right is St. Andrew's, tenderly cared for by the Redundant Churches Fund, possessing probably the finest Saxon tower in Northumberland, typically ladened with good old Hadrianic masonry; see the coffin lids incorporated into the outer face of the north transept wall (though the best have been removed). A little further along the by-way lies St Peter's still functioning as a place of worship in this heavenly place:

St Andrew's Bywell

predominantly a thirteenth century structure though the nave harbours Early Norman work. Having savoured this tranquil spot, backtrack to Bywell Bridge.

Follow the minor road leading north-east beside the river-bank. After a little over a third of a mile seek the ladder-stile on the left giving access to Bywell Haughs, liable to be cultivated. Traverse the field half right to a second ladder-stile secreted within bushes. The ensuing field may also be under plough, so follow the fence right, then at the corner rise to the stile in the hedge. Entering a great sweeping pasture, continue on a north-easterly line crossing a fence stile, ascend the bank to its brow. Scanning across the Tyne vale from this point Cherryburn overtops a green barn at Eltringham. Pass through the gateway in the hedge crossing the ridge, descend the pasture ridge to the stile/bridge spanning humble West Dean. Rise up the pasture beside the hedge to a stile on the left, then ascend the steeper pasture bank to enter Ovington at a stile beside a cottage. Go right passing the Highlander Inn (Newcastle Breweries), a splendid place of refreshment, displaying the welcoming 'open all day' banner. Pass (or enter!) the Ship Inn and Domingo's Pizzeria Restaurant. At the bend go straight ahead into St Andrews Lane by the Social Club. There's no denying Ovington offers choice for refreshment. Within thirty yards a well used and signposted footpath diverges left at a gateway, picking a direct course across cultivated land. Pass a ceramic trough to reach a stile at the far side of the second arable field. Continue diagonally across the next arable field to a stile in the north-east corner, follow the hedge via two further stiles to enter the scrub at the brink of Whittle Dene. At this point the walk marries with the WALL WALK, in prompt descent, latterly aided by steps to the iron footbridge over Whittle Dene Burn. Go right, down the valley midst delightful woodland rich in ground flora and bird song. At Eddybroth Well (pool with seat) the WALL WALK diverges up the slope left, however, this walk continues down the main valley path, via the ruined

The ruins of Whittle Dene Mill

16

Retreat homes in Whittle Dene

(though stabilised) Whittle Dene Mill. Wend through the quaint glade of tiny timber and brick dwellings. Vacate the woodland at the kissing-gate. The valley path passes down the meadow to a ladder-stile where the pasture 'bottle-necks'. Pass further chalet retreats to eventually reach the wall-stile onto the street in Ovingham, close to the church.

As is the quirky pattern of Northumbrian speech where a place-name includes 'ingham', this is pronounced 'injum', here giving 'Ovinjum', which is curiously similar to Birmingham, colloquially pronounced 'Brummijum'. Go left, then right down the village road as to Ovingham Bridge. As a final moment's quiet reflection briefly divert to inspect St Mary's church with its tall late Saxon tower, reminiscent of St Andrews at Bywell. Here the better touches are from the thirteenth century, notably the long chancel and transepts lit by slender lancets. Thomas Bewick is buried here. Continue down to the Tyne where pedestrians are given the security of their own bridge on stilts beside the road bridge back to the under used Riverside Park.

from CORBRIDGE ─────────────────────────

6 mile circular walk featuring:
Aydon Castle, Halton Castle and Onnum Roman Fort

Onnum from the vallum on Down Hill

> START grid ref. NY 994647

A walk to savour the drama of Aydon Castle, widely regarded as the finest example of a thirteenth century manor house in England. Rising beyond to view Halton Castle, a sumptuously embellished peel tower-turned-farmhouse, the walk culminates at Halton Chesters, Onnum Roman Fort, the fifth fort along the Wall, returning via Stagshaw Bank, scene of large 'fairs' from Saxon times.

Begin either from the centre of Corbridge by walking up Princes Street or from St Helen's Lane. Follow the pavement along Aydon Road. This pavement ceases above Jameson Drive. Shortly cross the A69. Turn left into the modified bridle-way which runs along a fenced passage adjacent to the new road cutting. This kinks right, rejoining the old path, then rises to a bridle-gate. Ascend the Gallow Hill pasture, follow the right-

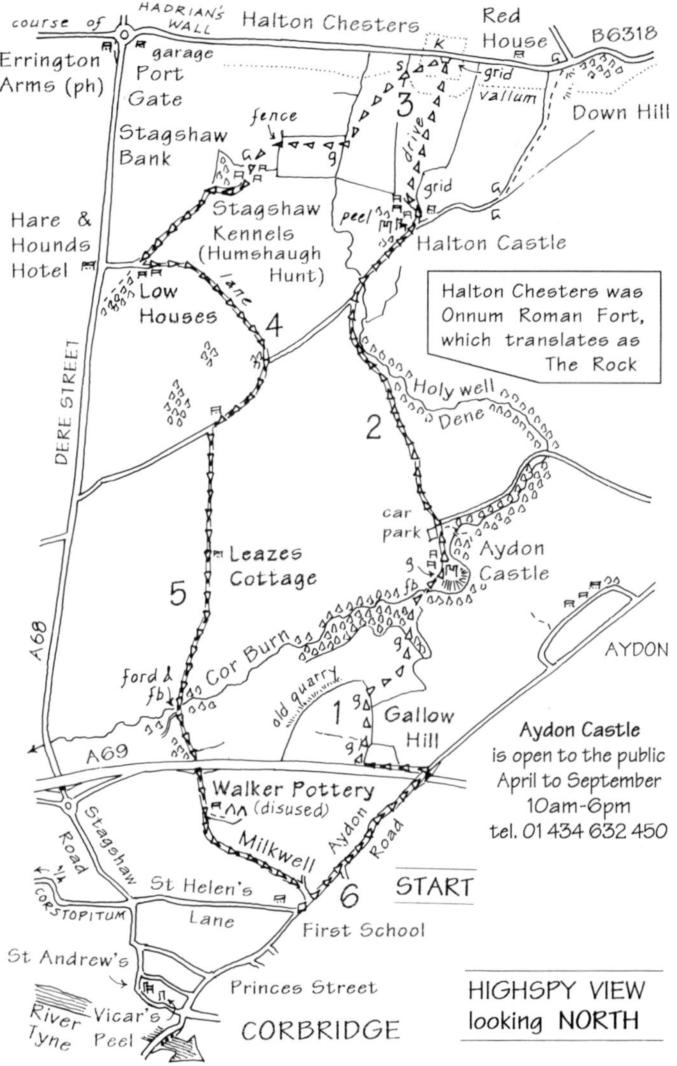

course of HADRIAN'S WALL
Halton Chesters
Red House
B6318
Errington Arms (ph)
garage
Port Gate
K
grid
vallum
Down Hill
fence
3
drive
Stagshaw Bank
g
grid
Hare & Hounds Hotel
Stagshaw Kennels (Humshaugh Hunt)
peel
Halton Castle
lane
Low Houses
4
Halton Chesters was Onnum Roman Fort, which translates as The Rock
Holy well
Dene
2
DERE STREET
car park
Aydon Castle
Leazes Cottage
g
fb
5
AYDON
A68
Cor Burn
old quarry
ford fb
1
g
Gallow Hill
g
g
Aydon Castle is open to the public April to September 10am-6pm tel. 01 434 632 450
A69
Walker Pottery (disused)
Milkwell
Aydon Road
Stagshaw Road
St Helen's Lane
START
6
CORSTOPITUM
First School
St Andrew's
Princes Street
River Tyne
Vicar's Peel
CORBRIDGE
HIGHSPY VIEW looking NORTH

hand hedge to a second bridle-gate. Note the novel pulley weight in a rustic length of fence. The path curves down to a bridle-gate yielding entry into a larch wood. The path, prone to be muddy, leads through to the Cor Burn. Beware : for above the stream the path has been eroded by the uprooting of storm damaged trees. Descend to the simple footbridge, in a charming dell pungent with wild garlic.

The presence of a defended house is kept a distant notion until the path mounts the steep bank, latterly in a cobbled hollow-way, whereupon the huge masonry and high walls gather defiantly above the path. The buttressed walls stand perilously close to the brink of the deep Cor Burn valley, woods ringing with the call of jackdaws. Go through the bridle-gate, approaching the house via the main gateway arch in the curtain wall. Aydon Castle is in the care of English Heritage which is working on a continual programme of fabric consolidation: entry fee at the shop (coffee). Devote a full hour to tour the whole building; closed during winter months. The name Aydon appears to mean 'hay meadow'.

Follow the farm track to its junction with the minor road next to the Castle visitors' car park. Take this minor road (north) for a mile to reach Halton Castle. At the green, step aside to visit the small church. By the path masquerading as a gravestone remains a Roman altar; it certainly makes a superior bird-bath!

Rodney Busby acts as sentry to Aydon Castle's vaulted tower, situated at the northern extremity of the outer courtyard

The imposing southern
aspect of Aydon Castle
overlooking Cor Burn

   This seventeenth century church replaced a Norman
chapel on the same site. In the church note the altar
in the chancel styled as a Roman temple, and the tablet,
above the pulpit, to the Victorian minister George Hodgson.
By quaint coincidence he was born Christmas Day 1821, and
died Easter Day 1886. From the fourteenth century Halton
Castle was the home of the Carnaby family, of London's
Carnaby Street fame. This family succeeded the ill-fated

Aydon Castle's eastern aspect

de Reymes at Aydon Castle, the estate inherited in 1751 via marriage to Sir Edward Blackett from Matfen, whose ancestors live here to this day.

To view the considerable vallum embankments on Down Hill, take the farm lane leading east from the green, past the cottages. This leads via sheep pens and a gate into an overgrown lane and used as a rubble dumping ground! From the gate at the end of the lane ascend the pasture, drift away from the wall to see the vallum. Unfortunately it has been quarried where the track crosses. Advance to the road from the gate. Go left, along the none too generous grass verges, to the cattle-grid entrance to the Halton Castle estate.

The main route lies along the Halton Castle drive, by the attractive horse watering-pond. Take the farm lane, adorned with 'private road' board, which leads via a farm cottage and cattle-grid to the unenclosed farm road. This leads straight up the pasture to the main

Halton Castle from the churchyard

road entrance. Divert immediately left via the kissing-gate, sign 'Fox and Hounds Inn Stagshaw 3/4'. The footpath crosses the irregular surface of the south-west corner of the fort to a ladder-stile. Cross the arable field slanting down to a bridle-gate in the boggy hollow. Ascend the pasture to a horse-jump stile, slant half left to a gate into the yard of Stagshaw Kennels, ever alert, the barks confirming this to be the home of Humshaugh Hunt Foxhounds. You will not slip through unheeded! Follow the access lane to the open common of Stagshaw Bank former scene of markets for the farming community either side of the Roman line, a major focus made convenient by Dere Street and Wade's Military

Road. The potholed track leads beyond Low Houses to The Fox and Hounds Hotel, a smart establishment thoroughly modernised, prepared to serve walkers once bereft of muddy boots. Strategically sited to draw custom from the great sheep and cattle fairs, now a distant folk memory - it stands at the south entrance to the common.

Return to Low Houses, forking right, down the rough tracked lane, to join the Halton road. Continue south, forking left at the ensuing junction passing the curious trimmed holly at Leazes Cottage. Descend to the footbridge beside the Cor Burn road-ford: the road slips through the great concrete A69 overpass and passes the old Walker Pottery. The three huge beehive brick kilns are a rare survival, view with caution. Follow Milkwell Lane to its junction with Aydon Road to conclude the walk into Corbridge.

Beehive brick kiln at the former Walker Pottery

24

Humshaugh Foxhounds 'at home'

The lane by Leazes Cottage

from ST.OSWALD'S ———————————————————

5 mile circular walk featuring:
River North Tyne, Chesters Roman Bridge, Brunton Turret,
Wall and Fallowfield

Limestone quarry below Brady's Crag

> **START** grid ref. NY 937694

Park on the B6318 at the Heavenfield lay-by beside the wooden cross to St.Oswald, approximately 1½ miles east of Chollerford Bridge. From the gate cross the pasture upon the track to St Oswald's chapel. Before 1879 the parish, comprising the townships of Bingfield, Cocklaw, Fallowfield, Hallington, Port-gate and Wall was called St Johnlee. The original church was built upon the site of a momentous battle in 635 A.D., between Oswald the Christian King of Northumbria and Cadwalla, the heathen leader of British tribes. Prior to this event Northumbria had been divided into two kingdoms, Deira

St. Oswald's
Chapel and the
Heavenfield Cross

and Bernicia. Deira was ruled by Oswald's uncle Edwin, who was converted to Christianity by Paulinus in 627 A.D., whilst Bernicia was ruled by Eanfrid, Oswald's brother. Cadwalla made war with Northumbria, confronted and slew Edwin, his son Osric, and Eanfrid, both the latter having renounced Christianity. So when Oswald became King he rallied forces, raised a rude wooden cross as a standard, and triumphed in Christ's name at Heavenfield (Heaven's Field).   Tradition holds this to have been an important moment for the flowering of Christianity in Britain: the church erected here by the monks of Hexham became the fountainhead for the proliferation of places of worship throughout the kingdom and beyond. Dating from 1737 the present building has services that, understandably, only take place during the warmer summer months.

Pass through to a stile in the northern corner of the churchyard, descend the succeeding pasture on line for the stile in the corner of the field. Negotiate the boggy ground to join a track descending past Brady's Crag. Slip through a gap in the hedge left, cross the stile, then angle right, round the hedge corner. The Pathfinder map implies a death defying 'dog-leg' course through the limestone quarry: be re-assured the footpath was long ago re-routed, so keep right guided by the barbed fence protecting the quarry edge from wayward sheep, cattle and walkers! Pass by the impressive, though crumbling, triple-arch lime kiln. Curving left below the quarry descend to a stile/bridle-gate: enjoy the view over Cocklaw Farms East and West, with its ruined peel tower. Descend the steep, spoil scarred, bank to a stile/gate. The path maintains company with the right-hand hedge to the gate and ensuing arable field. Join the road at a gate with footpath sign 'Heavenfield 1¼'. Follow the road left under the old railway bridge to the Bingfield road junction. Then left on the A6079. Across the field to

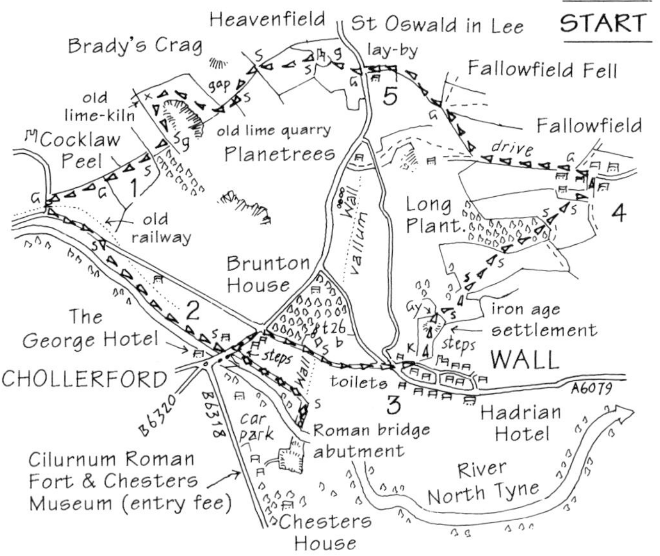

the left notice the lime-kilns, formerly connected to their quarry by aerial ropeway: burnt lime was loaded onto goods wagons for transportation to estates through the North Tyne valley.

After 300 yards descend the steps right. Follow the path downstream beside the river North Tyne, mindful that any anglers you meet, or for that matter are un-aware of on the river-bank, are also pursuing a quiet recre-ational experience and will not appreciate raucous walkers. Proceed quietly to the steps onto Chollerford Bridge.

Either cross the bridge, perhaps making the George Hotel a port of call. The old public bar rather sur-prisingly has survived the glitz of the hotel develop-

The old station
platform at Chollerford

ment making it a regular rambler's rest despite the fact that the principal clientele are gleaned from clean-heeled Wallsters. Continue 800 yards along the pavement beside the B6318 to include Chesters Museum and Cilurnum Roman Fort as profitable add-itions to the day's itinerary: when retraced, this spur adds a full mile. English Heritage runs a pleasant cafe 'Lucullus Larder', together with the usual shop facility, in all a package not to be dismissed lightly.

An appealing alternative is to visit the Roman Wall bridge abutment on the east side of the North Tyne. The access path descends steps opposite the point where the walk emerges onto Chollerford Bridge. Passing the decaying railway carriage, follow the fenced passage beside the former North Tyne Railway, veering right when the line of the wall is encountered. Gently descend to the quiet riverside and embowered site of the east abutment of the Roman North Tyne bridge; there is also evidence of a mill used to harness the river's oft powerful flow. Across the river the super de luxe Cilurnum bathhouse is clearly in view adjacent to the corresponding ramped bank formed to

Chesters Roman bridge abutment

assist in throwing the Roman wall bridge with chariot way high over the river. Should time be of essence make neither detour, and make haste along the road to the village of Wall, lured, perhaps by the prospect of refreshment at the Hadrian Hotel. Leaving Chollerford Bridge

River North Tyne from the western abutment ramp of Chesters Bridge eastward notice, left, the old station transformed into a private residence beside the lost railway. The route advances beyond the garage to the cross-roads at Low Brunton, where a water-wheel and gearing are attractively displayed. Follow the A6079 once more, making the obligatory diversion left after 300 yards to visit Brunton turret 26b and the length of attached wall, the finest composite survival east of Knag Burn (Housesteads). Continue the 800 yards by the main road forking left into Wall village.

Village pump,
The Green, Wall

You may wish to glance left within the square Green at the heart of the village, with 'island' cottages, water pump and the late Victorian Gothic church. Within St.George's Church hangs a particularly beautiful screen and an east window depicting Northumbrian saints.

Departing from the village via its eastern exit, take the footpath signed 'Fallowfield 3/4'. From the kissing-gate ascend the steep bank to inspect the intriguing Iron Age settlement site on School Hill. One might say the settlement has gravitated down the slope. Perhaps there was a settlement here before the Romans imposed their rule, the native Brits retiring to the comparative security of the camp at times of harassment. With the demise of Roman adminis-tration, this obviously agreeable location attracted the re-establishment of an expanded homestead. In medieval times Wall was a defended township, with the four points of access to the rectangular Green sealed from marauding Scots rustlers and reivers, which eventually evolved into the present-day village, never again needing to resort to the earthwork.

The footpath passes through a gateway in the bounding wall. Cross the stile right, then proceed south beneath the wall to veer left at the corner, rising to a passage to a stile. Ascend the pasture diagonally to a stile into Long Plantation. Prone to being over-grown in places, the path ascends the southern flank of the wood to a stile. Exit into pasture, maintaining course to the stile into a shelter belt at Fallowfield Farm. Go right then left along the farm lane to join the main road through the town-ship. Follow this left, along the unenclosed drive; the WALL WALK is co-incident as far as the drive to Crag House. Continue round the bend, via cattle-grids and gates returning, latterly as a lane, to the Heavenfield lay-by, journey's end.

from FOURSTONES ___________________________________

5¼ mile circular walk featuring: Stanegate Roman road,
the Iron Age encampment on Warden Hill
and 'Meeting of the Waters'
the confluence of the North and South Tyne.

Warden Hill from Walwick

START grid ref. NY 863680

Park in the broad lower part of the lane in the older end of Fourstones village. Walk up the road to the footpath sign 'Little Whinny Hill ½' directing right. Pass the cottages to a field-gate thereon advance with the wall on the right.

Fifty yards short of the next wall gate, notice the shelf merging from the left, plausibly a portion of the Stanegate, the Roman military corridor established seventy years in advance of the more illustrious mural frontier. This is a rare revelation of that 'stone road', now inconsequential in appearance. Lend a little imagination to conjure up the scene, nearly two millennia ago, when this was an important legionary highway.

From the ensuing gate advance to a wall stile, now turn sharp right keeping company with the right-hand wall along the discernible bridle-track. The Stanegate crosses quite imperceptibly, traversing the foot of the long gorsy slope to the left, bound for a lost ford of the North Tyne and ultimately

HIGHSPY VIEW looking EAST

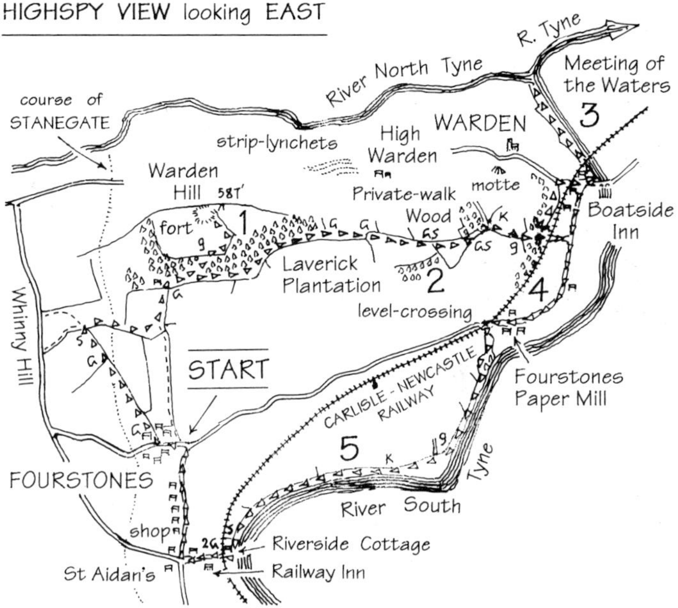

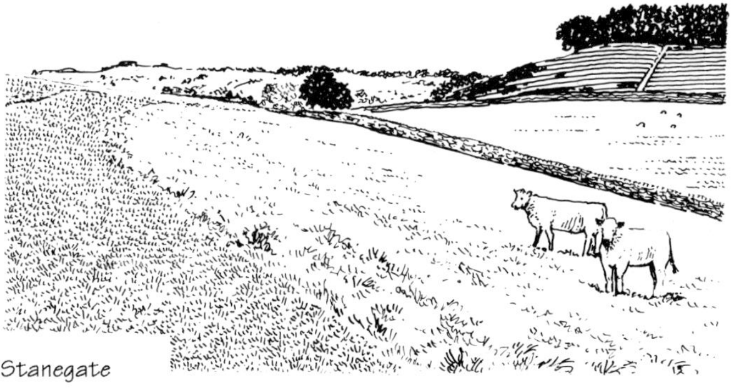

The name 'Fourstones' is intriguing being similar to Featherstone, which also appears to refer to standing stones, though in neither case are there megaliths to corroborate the place-name cryptic.

Stanegate

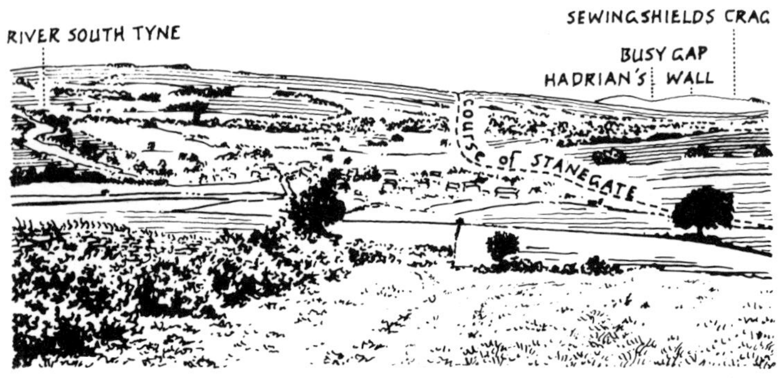

Fourstones from where the two bridleways merge

Corbridge. Follow the slightly sunken track-way through the gorse passing the wall-end. Keep on a contouring line till nearing the rising wall. Follow the wall till it merges with a second bridle-way ascending directly from Fourstones.

On reaching a gate adjacent to a remote cottage, follow the track-way sweeping right, guided by a blue waymark post. Accompany the wall to a fork, take the spur bridle/footpath route to the summit of Warden Hill: ascend through Laverick Plantation to a bridle-gate, follow the wall right, then climb beside the rising wall left on a footpath (which has no continuation beyond the summit) to reach the summit plateau. Tour the perimeter of the hill-fort, with its shallow stony double rampart, to enjoy the view over the North Tyne valley towards the village of Wall. To the north Chesters House can readily be identified.

The name Warden means 'look-out' and no finer vantage exists to survey activity within the twin valley corridors of North and South Tyne: the Normans later transferring the station to the motte at the foot of the south-east slope, more intimate with the valley scene. Obscured behind the wall is the old O.S. column [B.M.6662] marking the 587 foot summit,

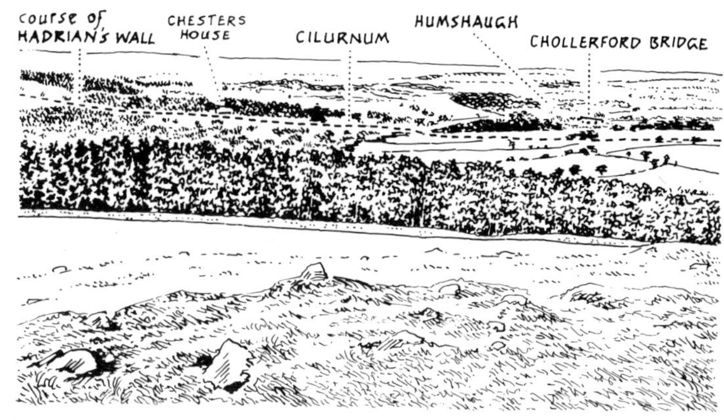

Iron Age entrenchments on Warden Hill

made 'out of bounds' by the defiant though *passe* 'Private Road' notice on the gate.

Retrace your steps down through Laverick Plantation; Laverick means 'outlying farm frequented by larks'. Bear sharp left along the original bridle-way which leads down to a field-gate exit of the woodland. Glance west up the South Tyne valley to Tindale Fells, the northern prow of the Pennines. Contour with the hedge then fence to a gate thus switching sides of the field boundary. Continue to a gate/ stile; henceforward the path descends more purpose- fully as it is drawn into a lane. After the gate/stile DO NOT be lured left within the lane (this is private); instead pass through the kissing-gate right. Bearing in mind that this is a bridle-way, precisely how would the horse get through? Descend the pasture beside the hedge/ fence to a bridle-gate entering a sunken passage within the woodland approaching the old railway cottages.

Should you wish to hasten back to Fourstones then simply head down to the level - crossing (facing ladder-

Laverick Plantation

stiles) to join the minor road, going right for Fourstones Paper Mill. To visit the Boatside Inn and the Tyne waters-meet, go left behind the cottage upon a very confined path soon coming tight beside the railway fence, eventually drifting left through a wild patch to join the minor road. Go right, under the railway bridge to reach the Boatside

Boatside Inn

River North Tyne approaching watersmeet

Inn: excellent food but currently no indoor facilities for children.

To visit the confluence of the North and South Tyne, pass down the lane signposted 'Meeting of the Waters' to the left of the bridge. Keep right of the cottage to the wall steps close to the bridge arch. Go left, passing under the metal railway bridge, and past the line of a former rail bridge, its piers still visible in the river. Winding through the light scrub the path terminates abruptly at the con-fluence, where each river tumbles over it rocky bed into a broad pool. The water level was quite low when I visited with my family; my children were able to explore the boulders, but this will not always be possible. Curiously we detected a strong salty tang to the air, strange as Tynemouth is thirty miles distant. Return by the Tyne Watersmeet Fishery hut (life-belt attached) and the Boatside Inn, heading west upon the pavement.

Approaching Fourstones Paper Mill (established in 1763) the pavement is lost; just prior to the level-crossing find the sign-posted footpath left 'Fourstones 1¼, Allerwash 2½'. The path leads via a narrow concrete walkway beside the fence to the riverbank. An attractive path ensues till drawn briefly away from the bank at a hand-gate, short-cutting the river bend through broom bushes and beside a wall to a kissing-gate. Thereafter the path hugs the riverbank. Here my son Daniel (ever the keen-eyed naturalist) spotted a stoat killing a rabbit and a heron in lazy flight: quiet walkers can catch nature off guard.

The path crosses the well-tended lawn of Riverbank Cottage, sensitively and imaginatively modernized. Bear right to the level-crossing, follow the road uphill past the Railway Inn to the road junction. Notice the unusual weather-boarded parish church, St. Aidan's, left and the post office-cum-general dealer shop ahead. Go right to complete the walk along the pavement.

St. Aidan's, Fourstones

SIMONBURN

from BROCOLITIA

6 mile circular walk featuring :
Simonburn Castle, Teppermoor Hill
and Brocolitia Roman Fort
and Mithreum

Simonburn Village Shop

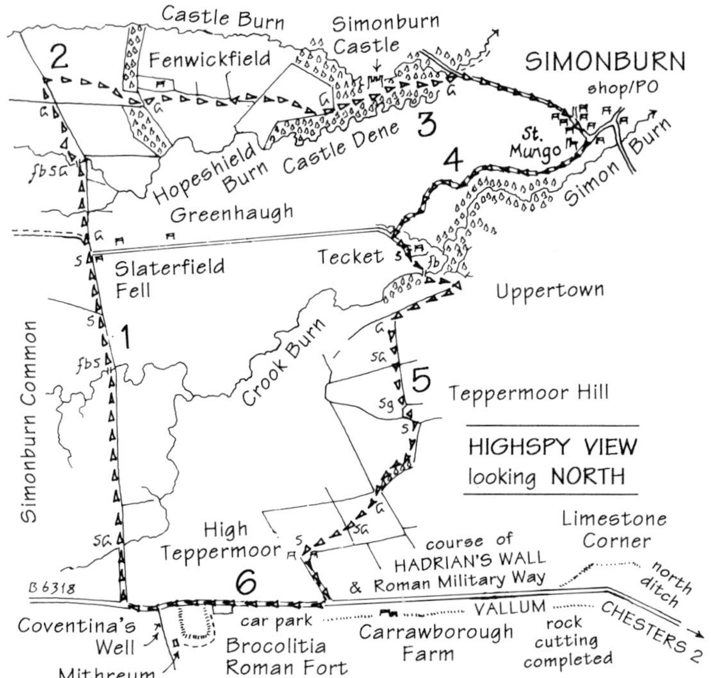

START grid ref. NY 860712

Leave the Brocolitia car park left, on the non-too generous verges of the B6318. Pass the featureless plateau of Brocolitia, awaiting contemporary excavation. In the meantime nature's archaeologists, moles, are giving the sub-soil a thoroughly good turning over. The shallow rigs on the west bank obscure the fort's vicus. The course of the Roman Military Way is discernible approaching a metal gate in the valley bottom wall. Below this, in the marshy hollow, lies the recondite remains of Coventina's Well, excavated by John Clayton in the hoard-hunting fashion of his Victorian age. A rich cache of offertory coins, spanning the full span of Roman occupation, indicate this Celtic deity held an enduring reverence, perhaps as a bode of deliverance from this bleak place.

Boundary dyke at the crossing of Hopeshield Burn

Ascend the hill to take your own deliverance from the traffic terrorised highway, right, along the bridle-lane, signposted 'Greenhaugh 1', which advances to a ladder-stile. To remain dry-shod follow the bank left of the track, duly descending to a ladder-stile and plank footbridge spanning Crook Burn. Notice the stone sheep dip just beyond. Subsequently ascend beside the wall, latterly fence, to cross a fence-stile, from where is the vestige of a hedge confirming the existence of a drove-way lane on the rise to a stile at Slaterfield Fell (farm). The curious eye-catching lodge, undergoing some renovation, though probably built as a barn is dignified by its matching triple-pinnacled gable-ends. The owner is apparently a keen huntsman, as the Humshaugh Hunt were meeting at his door the following day to my February visit. Follow the Stoop-rigg farm lane north passing through the gate on the right-hand side of the cattle-grid, diverging where it turns left. Continue down the pasture, beside the recently re-built field wall, crossing a burn, en route to a hollow-way leading to the plank bridge over Hopeshield Burn. Angle left to climb the stile adjacent to the galvanised gate. Notice the slack coal exposed in the steep burn banks, notably upstream and the ox-bow in the meandering burn.

Follow the track heading north-west for no more than 100 yards before switching right - little evidence of bridle-way on the ground, nor wall. Advance north to a gate in a new fence on the crest of the rig. Continue only a matter of 120 yards before turning right through the gap by the vestige enclosure wall. Proceed to the space between the conifer shelter-belt plantations where aim for the southern (righthand) gate. Pass the

Simonburn Castle, ruined thirteenth century peel tower

cottage and outbuildings of Fenwickfield (pronounced 'fenikfield'), joining the unenclosed access track which winds pleasantly down to a gate into Castle Dene Plantation. The road shortly passes the unheralded pile of Simonburn Castle. A cursory perambulation of this ruined thirteenth century peel reveals the lancet windows to the submerged tunnel-vaulted basement and walls up to eight feet thick, to this ancient defended retreat of the Herons of Chipchase. Originally four storeys high, Simonburn Tower was rebuilt in 1766, with twin turrets at the angles as a folly by the Allgoods of Nunwick, later torn to its present decrepitude by treasure seekers.

The concrete road pitches down to a gate and subsequent lane junction in the valley bottom. Go right, up the road to enter Simonburn, the estate village to Nunwick Hall. Simonburn Village Shop/Post Office (open weekdays 9-5 a.m., Wednesday and Saturday 9-12 a.m., closed Sunday) lies up the side lane left. Beyond the discreet telephone kiosk pass along the green to the handsome lych-gate to St.Mungo's Church (see below).

Largely re-built in 1860, though incorporating earlier elements, note the Saxon cross-shaft in the porch and the defaced Cuthbert Ridley monument of 1625 in the church, where the floor has the weird sensation of dipping towards the altar.

Beyond the lych-gate bear right up the lane passing the church car park, ascending the hill, with fine views back towards Chipchase Castle. The lane winds up to a cottage where bear left along the approach lane to Tecket Farm. Strategically perched on the narrow tip of the ridge there lurks a peel tower in the masonry of the farmhouse, though this is beyond our gaze, for the path directs right at a ladder-stile immediately short of the barns. Follow the farmyard fence to its corner where descend the steep bank diagonally left guided by waymarking to a footbridge over Crook Burn. The path mounts left beside a fence rising past a huge boulder and above a hollow-way to a hand-gate approaching Uppertown farmhouse via a gate. However, turn acutely right (south-west) to pass the new barn following the lane to a gate. Here bear left beside the rivulet, ascending, via a fence-stile/gate to a ladder-stile/bridle-gate. The path mounts the short bank curving right to a ladder-stile on Teppermoor Hill. This is quite the most scenic moment on the tour, with the North Tyne valley superbly displayed across the northern arc of the view, a mass of fields and shelter belts leading the eye towards the Simonside Hills and The Cheviots. While to the south east Limestone Corner is the prominent scarp, where ran Hadrian's Wall, its unfinished north ditch meriting a visit when the walk is complete.

Advance to the plantation bearing right upon a track passing through a gate at the end, continuing as an unenclosed track leading through the middle of the ensuing pasture crossing a ladder-stile. Approaching High Teppermoor keep right of the first barns angling left through a muddy access short of the farmhouse, where cross the ladder-stile onto the farm lane. Follow this south to join the main road, turning right to complete the walk.

ROMAN EFFECTS

With ten minutes to spare walkers may productively use the time in strolling down the pasture below the barren plateau of Brocolitia to view the Mithreum, exhibited to face the harsh elements with replica features. The wet setting which preserved the original monument continues to ensure that visitors need to be well shod to cope with the muddy environs.

East of Brocolitia the B6318 runs, as a result of the unfortunate work of eighteenth century military road engineers, upon the course of both the Roman Wall and Military Way. The vallum faired better and unlike the incomplete Roman endeavour of the north ditch at Limestone Corner, huge blocks of Whin Sill were arranged along the rim of the vallum ditch. Evidently having prized the basalt from the hard bedrock they were content to leave it thus.

The rock-cut vallum directly
south of Limestone Corner
- task accomplished

GRINDON LOUGH 6

from LADYSHIELD

5½ mile circular walk featuring:
Busy Gap, Vercovicium Roman Fort and Grindon Lough

View from King's Hill to
Housesteads, Hotbank and Winshields Crags

START grid ref. NY 816678 | Skirting the Knag Burn basin this route not only provides an enlarged perspective of Vercovicium but also has the distinction of following both Stanegate and Hadrian's Wall.

Park on the verge near the modernised cottage ¾ mile west of the Grindon Hill cross-roads. Pass through the gate immediately west of the cottage. Follow the right-hand wall north on a track, which bears left in the hollow sweeping round to a gate. Pass an old lime-kiln whence bear right to a gate, aiming for the isolated barn at Grindon Mill Hills: the right-of-way takes an unnecessary gated route through the yard; less disruption would be caused by glancing by on the east side.

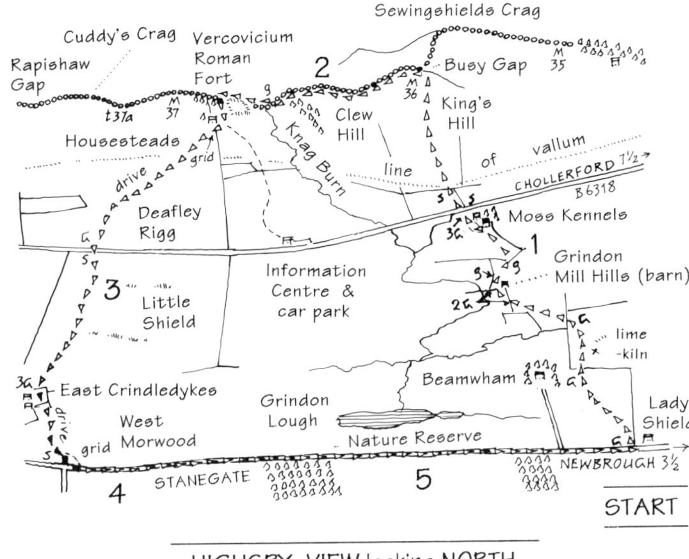

HIGHSPY VIEW looking NORTH

The path advances away from the track right via two narrow gates. Cross a hollow to rise beside the wall to Moss Kennels Farm. Keeping left through the yard, via three gates, to reach the B6318 road, cross directly and climb the ladder-stile to commence a direct ascent of King's Hill via a second ladder-stile. The path crosses the vallum at this point. Reaching the brow of King's Hill, said to be named after the legendary King Arthur, the path arrives upon King's Wicket. The depression immediately north oddly omitted from O.S. mapping, is known as Busy Gap, the infamous line of advance and retreat of Moss Troopers and Border Reivers. Holding to the line of the Roman Wall the walk goes west over Clew Hill, by the neat wall. Passing through the pine copse on Kennel Crags follow the splendid length of reconstructed Wall down to the Knag Burn 'gate' flanked by guard-houses, with an adjacent Wall culvert. Go through the narrow gate following the Wall left. Ascend the scarp to pass Vercovicium's northern gateway, set on strong foundations, to reach steps onto the Wall. Cross directly over, do not follow the inviting path through Housesteads Wood. Pass the fort's west gate-way, descend beside a rack of mortar cocktails, experimental mixtures concocted by English Heritage to help in the quest for a durable and aesthetically sympathetic material for future Wall consolidation. Should you wish to examine the interior of the fort, you are obliged to purchase tickets, at modest outlay, from

Hadrian's Wall rising from the Knag Burn culvert to Vercovicium

Housesteads Museum which houses an interesting exhibition relating to Vercovicium.

Follow the Housesteads access road via the cattle-grid, leading to the B6318 on Deafley Rigg. It is interesting to see in post-Roman times, how the vallum below Housesteads, across ½ mile of the dip slope west of Knag Burn, was absorbed into a series of cultivation terraces.

From the entrance gate cross the busy road, climb the re-located ladder-stile and descend into the shallow valley, initially accompanying the foundations of an old wall. Ascend the opposing bank on a tractor track traversing the Little Shield ridge to East Crindledykes. Passing through the farmyard, via three gates, follow the access drive diverting to the wall-stile on the rise to the road. Go left upon the minor road, overlaying the Stanegate Roman Military Way, which pre-dates Hadrian's Wall by a full century. Grindon Lough is the main attraction along this normally quiet by-way: note the discreet wall plaque directly above the lake erected by Northumberland Wildlife Trust. From this point on Stanegate the sheet of water and growing marsh are seen in suitably distant grandstand fashion. Grindon Lough attracts a surprising diversity of bird-life from wild duck and geese to hen harriers and merlin.

Housesteads from the Northumberland Naturalist's Trust plaque overlooking Grindon Lough

from HOUSESTEADS

3 mile circular walk featuring:
Vercovicium Roman Fort, Milecastle 37, Cuddy's Crags
and the Roman Military Way

Rapishaw Gap

START grid ref. NY 794684

From the car park pass round the National Trust Information Centre accompanying the tourist path to Housesteads Museum. Ascend the terraced hillside. Should you wish to inspect Vercovicium Roman Fort purchase an access ticket at the museum. Continuing past the mortar racks and the west gate to reach the steps over the Wall, situated between the rounded corner of the

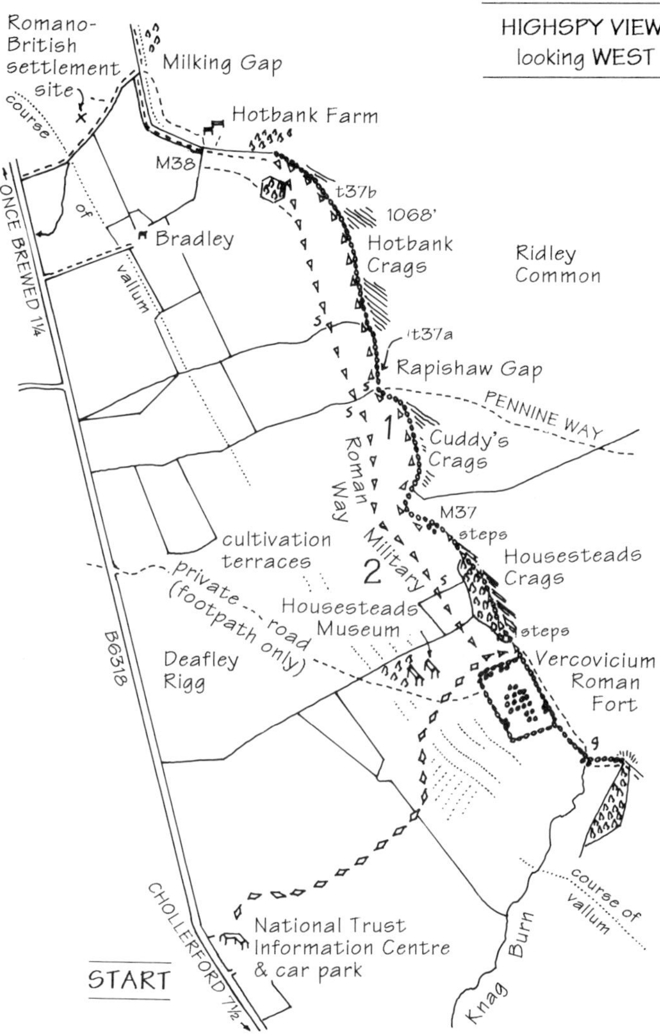
HIGHSPY VIEW
looking WEST
Romano-British settlement site
course of
Milking Gap
Hotbank Farm
M38
Bradley
vallum
ONCE BREWED 1¼
t37b
1068'
Hotbank Crags
Ridley Common
t37a
Rapishaw Gap
PENNINE WAY
Roman Way
Cuddy's Crags
1
M37
steps
Housesteads Crags
cultivation terraces
Military
2
Housesteads Museum
steps
Vercovicium Roman Fort
private road (footpath only)
B6318
Deafley Rigg
Knag Burn
course of vallum
National Trust Information Centre & car park
START
CHOLLERFORD 7½

Sewingshields Crag from Housesteads

fort and Housesteads Plantation. The walk pursues a westerly course on the south side of the Wall, ascending through the sycamore and pine wood with frequent glimpses right over the fluted pinnacles of dolerite that compose Housesteads Crag. Here the Whin Sill outcrops dramatically, giving an airy sensation to the view across the moorland to Broomlee Lough and the distinctive scarp of Sewingshields Crag. Leaving the wind-torn wood the path advances to Milecastle 37.

Hadrian's Wall switchback course on Housesteads Crag

Milecastle 37

The path proceeds via the stepped path into a hollow, then crosses Cuddy's Crags to enter Rapishaw Gap, joining the Pennine Way at a ladder-stile. Continue alongside the Wall over Hotbank Crags. There is little evidence of crags from the path, nor heat underfoot for that matter, possibly the name is akin to 'haut' in Haltwhistle, meaning 'high place', a topographically sound suggestion?

The Wall reverts to a mere 'wall': stop and enjoy the splendid prospect west over Crag Lough backed by Highshield Crags. Beyond is Once Brewed National Park Centre with the

The distinctive Clayton Wall running along the top of Hotbank Crags

View west from Hotbank Crags over Crag Lough to Winshield Crags

northern Pennine Fells as a backdrop across the South Tyne valley. Further along the craggy wall of the Whin Sill are Peel Crags, Steel Rigg and Winshields Crags. At 1132 feet above sea level it is the highest point on Hadrian's Wall. Backtracking above the hexagonal plantation, keep below the crest of the ridge. Accompany the obvious green way, once the Roman Military 'service' Way, a supply and auxiliary strata via between forts; not to be confused with the earlier Stanegate strata via or, indeed, Wade's Military Road constructed in the 1750s and now the B6318. The Roman Military Way returns, via stiles on a gently graded green carpet, to Vercovicium's west gate. If you purchased a ticket earlier you may now look over the fort. Vercovicium is the most impressively sited Wall fort, only rivalled in detail by Cilurnum and the Stanegate forts Corstopitum and to a lesser degree Vindolanda, which has a largely complete vicus. Housesteads has everything you would hope to see in a Hadrianic open-air exhibition. The museum, managed by the National Trust in association with English Heritage, is the first port of call: there is a charge for entry, even for the 'elite beat' twentieth century Wall legio. This five star, five acre fort contains a central headquarters building, commanding officers' house, twin barrack blocks, a hospital, latrines and granaries. Outside, on the southern approach, is evidence of an extensive vicus, the civilian settlement which flourished to service the garrison's needs. Below the vicus an extensive area of terracing strongly suggests that its inhabitants were encouraged to grow corn for the fort's granaries: excavations indicated that they were established during the third century, some having palisading. The lynchets will have continued to be cultivated through periods of comparative calm into medieval times, when the 'House' steading became established as more than just the summer shieling.

Roman Military Way leading east towards Vercovicium

HIGHSHIELD CRAGS 8

from ONCE BREWED

4 mile circular walk featuring:
Peel and Highshield Crags, Castle Nick, Sycamore Gap,
Milking Gap, Vindolanda Roman Fort and vicus

Crag Lough and Highshield Crags from Castle Gap

START grid ref. NY 753669

From the car park at the Northumberland National Park Centre, cross the B6318: keep alert and alive - not aloof - this road is notorious, for traffic zips along this switchback highway as if on a 'luge run'.

Ascend the minor road winding up past Peel Bothy towards the Steel Rigg car park, diverting right at the brow to join the path beside the Roman Wall. Looking east along the Whin Sill reveals one of the most exhilarating prospects Hadrian's Wall has to offer, an undulating scarp providing many memorable moments to savour. Passing through a kissing-gate the path swings round beside the Wall and descends into Peel Gap. Looking ahead eyes focus upon the pinnacled face of Peel Crags, a popular resort for rock-climbers who find that the secure holds offer good sport in the chimney rifts and pinnacle edges. The clear path descending to the foot of the crags from this spot is NOT a right-of-way. The Wall Walk crosses the paved causeway in Peel Gap adjacent to a recently re-consolidated irregular Milecastle. Evidently the Romans felt the natural breach in the Whin Sill needed extra surveillance so strengthened it by this supplementary guard post. Climb the steps among Peel Crags, broken out-cropping: notice the odd variety of mortar mixes at the top, the National Trust's experimentation to find the most durable and aesthetic composition to consolidate the Wall. Cross the step-stile. Proceed beside the Wall reconstructed by John Clayton's Chesters estate labour

Peel Bothy and Gap

force during the latter part of the nineteenth century. This has become the traditional image of the Wall, though the modern attempts at more durable construction ring truer to the original Roman pointing, witness Sycamore Gap. Visitors are more than ever discouraged to stride along the top of the Wall; in any case by so doing they miss the rare Roman swastika, situated between turret 39a and Cats' Stairs. Whether added by a legionary during original construction or later by an auxiliary, is not clear, but the sanskrit symbol was considered to bring prosperity and therefore 'good luck'. It remained 'in situ' because the lower three courses of the Wall survived stone robbers, lingering for centuries undisturbed beneath core rubble until the Victorian reconstruction.

Rodney standing beside the swastika stone

Descending via the ladder-stile in a minor weakness in the Sill, glance upon the spring spilling down Cats' Stairs, thought to be an allusion to wild cats. Continuing along the crest of the ridge the Wall diminishes to a low rubble shadow of recent glories.

The descent into Castle Nick re-kindles anticipation of great things afoot, and Milecastle 39 fully matches up to its setting. A square peg in a square hollow. Medieval shepherds' 'shielings' foundations lie beside the Wall on the top of the ensuing crest of Mons Fabricus. There is evidence that the milecastle was adapted for contemporary stock shelter too. The shielings will have nestled beside a wall of some height shielding from north-easterlies. Just beyond the shielings excavation has also revealed 'Broad Wall' foundations eschewed by legionary constructors of the 'Narrow Wall'.

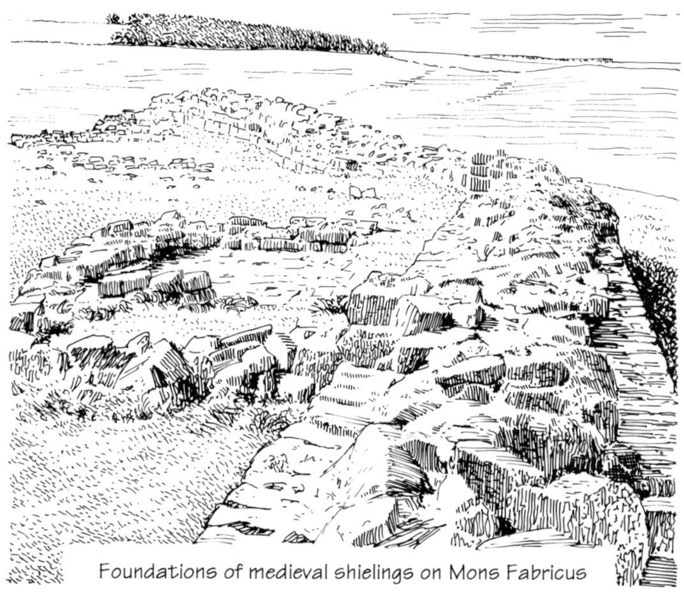

Foundations of medieval shielings on Mons Fabricus

The Wall Walk path descends a flight of steps into Sycamore Gap, with the ageing and stripling (in the tiny circular walled enclosure) trees. Walkers may curtail their adventure here returning along the Roman Military Way to regain the road via two ladder-stiles behind Peel Bothy.

Sycamore Gap from Mons Fabricus

From Sycamore Gap mount the steep bank on the north side of the Wall, which is lost at the next stile. The way is now set along the crest of Highshield Crags, with exciting, if not to stress perilous, views down the sheer face and into Crag Lough, popular haven for wild ducks, geese and swans. Entering a sycamore and pine wood descend via a ladder-stile, to meet the Hotbank Farm access track. Go right at the ladder-stile/gate in Milking Gap following the farm track through the

Highshield Crags from the marsh
of Crag Lough.   In the distance
Hadrian's Wall is seen rising
over Hotbank Crag

natural cutting, branching right (footpath sign).
Forty yards south of the sign survey the rough circle of
rocks in the pasture. These orthostats mark the site of
a Romano-British farmstead, thought to have been established during a settled period when stock-farming could
have co-existed with military control.

Romano-British farmstead near Milking Gap

The undefined path traverses the rough pasture to join the vallum and reaching the farthest wall corner crosses a ladder-stile into the neighbouring pasture beside the vallum. Proceed to a ladder stile onto the B6318, opposite the entrance to High Shield Farm. Follow the approach lane, keeping left round the buildings guided by waymarking via stiles to commence the long southerly descent of the pasture: notice the two 'Y'-shaped bields, wind-shelters for sheep. Lower down there is evidence of ridge and furrow cultivation, whilst at the foot of the field, right of the **stile/gate**, standing beside an even older burial mound is the Roman Milestone, one of only two in-situ along Stanegate. What marvellous fortune it has survived intact.

VINDOLANDA beckons: either go left to enter via Chester-holm Museum or right, pass Codley Farm ascending the rough tracked Stanegate lane, to the National Park car park. After parting with several denarii (pound coins) the superb vicus, fort and the Vindolanda Trust's famous Wall Re-construction may be explored.

One hundred yards beyond the entrance to the car park on Stanegate, opposite the Kingcairn track gate, take the step stile right. Traverse the pasture in a northerly direction descending into

Roman Milestone at Codley

the wooded dell. Cross the footbridge to negotiate stiles, ascend past an old lime-kiln and ruin, then cross the fence (stile) in the wall angle. Continue to the step-stile onto the B6318. Go left upon the meagre verge to conclude the walk, watchful of the speeding traffic.

from STEEL RIGG

7 mile circular walk featuring:
Housesteads Roman Fort and the Whin Sill escarpment
from Busy Gap to Peel Crags

Looking east along the Great Whin Sill from Steel Rigg

START grid ref. NY 751677

This elongated walk may not deliver the entire craggy spine of the Whin Sill, but succinctly bestows on the walker a distillation of the very essence of Wall Country. The walk exposes the full vigour of Whin Sill scenery combined with the finest stretches of consolidated Wall from Housesteads. Start from the Steel Rigg car park. Walk back onto the road turning right (north) descending to the ladder-stile/gate right; follow the track east beneath Hound Hill. Pass Peatrigg Plantation and Peatrigg, a black dutch barn, to a ladder-stile/gate: notice the traces of ridge and furrow in the pasture sloping to the south. Pass the Long Side barn to a ladder-stile adjacent to

Highshield Crags from Peatrigg

a sheep fold. The path bears half right crossing two modest footbridges and a stile, mindful to comply with the 'single file through the hay-crop' entreaty, to reach a further stile/gate. From this point the walk may be shortened. A right-hand turn through the gate leads along the track, through Hotbank Farm's gated yard to join the WALL WALK early at the site of Mile-castle 38 (see National Trust information panel). The walk bears left upon the tractor track. At the fork, take the right-hand branch along the ridge, passing a limestone quarry and collapsed lime-kiln, the double-arched structure illustrated below. At the next wall commiserate with any Pennine Wayfarers you may encounter at the ladder-stile; half of their thirteen mile

Double-arched lime-kiln

plod to Bellingham is enveloped within the oppressive monotony of Wark Forest, whereas your next five miles is one joyous scenic crescendo after another - the traverse of Ridley Common excepted, though that provides a fine view!

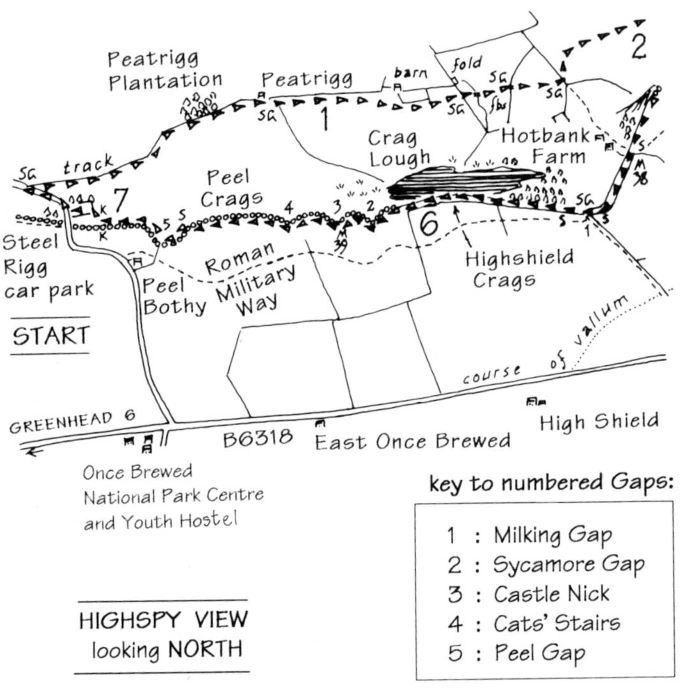

HIGHSPY VIEW
looking **NORTH**

key to numbered Gaps:

1 : Milking Gap
2 : Sycamore Gap
3 : Castle Nick
4 : Cats' Stairs
5 : Peel Gap

The eastward trek crosses rough pasture to King's Wicket, with the view of Housesteads Roman Fort and the craggy Whin Sill a constant fascination. Pass above the circular sheep fold (the place-name Steel Rigg could mean 'ridge with a circular fold') and through the isolated young conifer plantation via stiles. Bear right upon entry. Beyond this hazard the footpath descends via drainage ditches before mounting to the ladder-stile/wicket

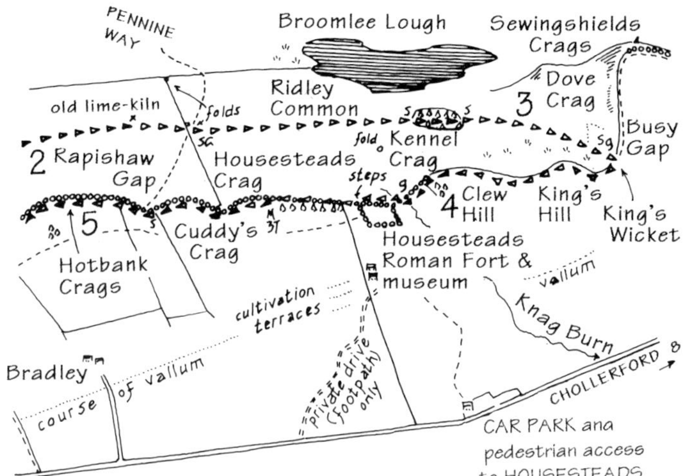

gate at King's Wicket above the Busy Gap enclosure earthwork. Compounding the Wall's north ditch this feature is of unclear date and purpose; if it had been stockaded it would appear to have made a useful corral. It is hard to imagine this nick as 'busy', there being little more than the faintest trod infiltrating to King's Wicket from the 'wastes'. Yet this weakness in the Sill was notorious in medieval times as the 'eye of the needle' access to the lush pastures and sheltered steadings of Tynedale for reiver sorties: this way moss troopers bent on theft came and went, returning to the vast northern wilds, droving their ill-gotten gains 'as from market'. A 'Busy Gap Rogue' was long used as a Geordie term of abuse.

Go left over King's Hill: is this a further allusion to the enigmatic Arthur, associated in local tradition with Sewingshields Crags? Advance beside the neat nine-teenth century field wall, clearly raised from remnant Wall stone and set upon the Roman kerb. Traverse the diminutive Clew Hill which would appear to mean 'ridge

King's Wicket

of the cleft', **descending to a ladder-stile entry into a fir plantation on Kennel Crag:** in common with most other Whin Sill hills, named after the farm for which it was pasturage, in this instance Moss Kennels.

Jubilation reigns at the next prospect, for, stretching across the broad mouth of the Knag Burn hollow, is the finest length of Wall yet beheld, dipping to a unique Roman gateway with flanking guardrooms. The wild lands to the north may look unpromising, inhospitable territory but bearing in mind Busy Gap's traffic, certainly from Roman times until the sixteenth century, this was an area alive with incursionaries: indeed, rather than control traffic direct from Vercovicium, perched strategically upon the scarp top, the Romans considered it sufficiently effective to marshal movement through this natural bottle-neck. Glance left down the valley to spot the crudely fenced Roman bath-house Well. This is the one instance on the whole frontier where the WALL WALK adopts the control or gateway created by the Roman engineers. Passing through, go left ascending the bank to follow Vercovicium's north wall, which doubled as the frontier Wall. Ascend the ramp leading past the north gateway (notice its strong foundations), continue beyond the rounded western corner of the fort to steps onto the Wall - a particularly fine vantage to comprehend the fort.

Take time to visit Housesteads Museum and purchase a ticket to inspect Vercovicium, arguably the most impressive of all Roman Wall forts. The WALL WALK has recently been re-routed via stiles off the top of the Wall within Housesteads Plantation, safely back from the exciting shattered basalt cliff. At Milecastle 37 notice the third century narrowing of the Wall gateway arch, and the Roman Military Way evident in the grass, only a matter of yards down the south slope. The WALL WALK clings to the consolidated Wall's side as it descends a flight of purpose cut steps, kinking through the unnamed nick before rising onto Cuddy's Crags: the view back is a famous camera composition. Cuddy, a

Hadrian's Wall sweeping across the Knag Burn valley

Buttressed Horreum (granaries) at Vercovicium

corruption of Cuthbert, has long been a common christian name in the area. St.Cuthbert was the seventh century Bishop of Lindisfarne, and patron saint of Northumberland.

The next sharp descent, with the Wall interrupted by crags, brings the WALL WALK into Rapishaw Gap, where the Pennine Way quits the Roman Wall, via a ladder-stile right. Crossing our own ladder-stile the WALL WALK traverses Hotbank Crags: no hypocaust to warm your feet as the name may imply. The view west, though not quite as extensive as Sewingshields, is nonetheless rapturous, leading the eye over Crag Lough to Highshield and Winshields Crags.

Southward the heather-clad Barcombe (pronounced 'bor-cum'), with the Long Stone miners' memorial visible, overlooks Chesterholm and Vindolanda, the central Stane-gate fort. Stanegate must have continued to function as both a civil and military trade and travel route throughout the Roman period. The four 'loughs' or Wall Country Lakes can also be spotted from this vantage: Grindon, Crag, Greenlee and Broomlee.

The exciting switchback course of Hadrian's Wall leading to Cuddy's Crags

On the descent to a stile the Wall is lost. Enter a small enclosure containing the outline of Milecastle, robbed to leave nought but the barest shadow of its curtain wall in the rough grass. The explanatory plaque refers to the inscribed stones found here; they recorded its construction by the second legion in the reign of Hadrian under the governorship of Platorius Nepos.

The north ditch re-emerges as the scarp slope eases below Hotbank Farm. The WALL WALK leads down to ladder-stiles at Milking Gap, where the Hotbank Farm access track slips through a narrow natural breach. Go left, ascending into the plantation via a ladder-stile climbing to the top of Highshield Crags.

All along the view is exhilarated by the bird's eye perspective on the choppy waters of Crag Lough, a wetland sanctuary where man's incursions are seldom felt, a happy home for swans and a diversity of ducks. As the Wall has not been

West along the Whin Sill from Highshield Crags

excavated along the crest of the cliff, one's attention is naturally rather warily focused on the drama of the basalt columns at one's feet. Crossing a stile the Wall re-emerges and anticipation mounts.

Above Sycamore Gap the National Trust has experimented with a cocktail of mortar mixes during the recent consolidation campaign in this sector. You may also have noticed their trial rack above Housesteads Museum. The old sycamore in Sycamore Gap is a distinctive feature of this section of the Wall. However, archaeologists could be forgiven for wanting to chop it down. The motivation for such drastic action lies hidden in its roots. When the debris was removed from the north side of the Wall, six to eight courses of undisturbed Roman masonry was revealed, including a surprising amount of Whinstone. This tiny section provides a unique view of the original structure and pointing of the Wall. Elsewhere the Wall has been 'gathered up' and reconstructed, apart from the lower two or three courses of 'Clayton Wall' - a prime example being on view along the crest of Peel Crags.

The WALL WALK climbs steeply onto Mons Fabricus where lie remains of medieval shielings and a fragment of Broad Wall kerbing. Descend into Castle Nick, where Milecastle 39 snugly rests. The Wall deteriorates to ragged rubble; the WALL WALK reaches a ladder-stile in a shallow dip in the ridge above the Cats' Stairs cleft. The Wall re-emerges to its fullest modern stature as a plume across the top of Peel Crags.

Approaching the site of turret 39a, keen eyed detection can locate the Roman swastika etched in a lower course of the Wall. The swastika, a Roman good luck emblem, occurs regularly in Roman artefacts such as glass and pottery, but is rare within the Wall's stonework.

The WALL WALK descends steeply through Peel Gap rising to accompany the Wall to Steel Rigg car park. Give one last long look back, on a memorable Wall and Whin Sill extravaganza.

from CHESTERHOLM

3¼ mile circular walk featuring:
Barcombe, Thorngrafton Common, Chainley Burn,
Vindolanda Roman Fort and Museum

Chesterholm Museum

| START grid ref. NY 774664 |

Park at the National Park car park to the east of Chesterholm (see Roman site layout plan by entrance). The course of Stanegate (oddly mis-spelt on Pathfinder maps as 'Stangate') defines the boundary of the National Park in this vicinity, placing the car park beyond its limits. Exit left ascending to the road junction; go left. A few yards short of the next junction cross the wall-stile right, footpath sign-posted Thorngrafton. Prior to embarking on the ascent be sure to divert left from the road junction to inspect the Crindledykes quadruple lime-kiln (see info. panel).

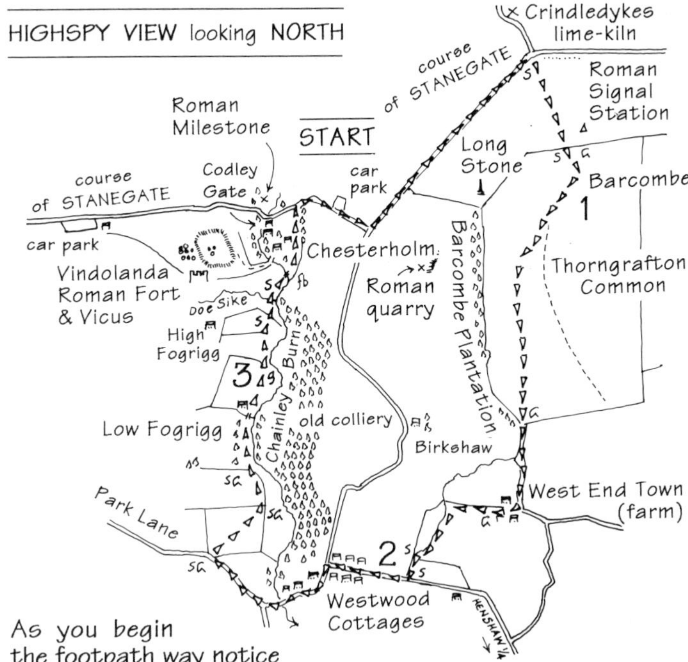

As you begin
the footpath way notice
the tunnel beneath the road and
old mine wagonway leading to it. The path inclines up the
heather-clad scarp venturing towards a wall squeeze-
stile, to the right of a gateway. All diversions from this
path confer no rights. Tempting us from the straight and
narrow is the Roman Signal Station crowned by the redundant O.S. triangulation column up to the left, a fine vantage
for the Whin Sill skyline and the beelining Stanegate
Roman road. Of even greater allure is the parade along the
scarp right beside the brink dyke to inspect the Long
Stone (find the cryptic etched arrow topped with the
initials TR). This latter, a prominent landmark, is said
to have been erected in the last century as a memorial
to nine colliers who lost their lives in a Chainley Burn

Mine accident. A finer viewpoint for Vindolanda does not exist. Beyond the cross-ridge wall the ridge steps down to a Roman quarry, where is etched a large phallic symbol, a prime example of Roman graffiti; the motif sought to bestow 'good fortune' on the fighting men of Vindolanda.

The Miners' memorial

Crindledykes lime-kiln

From the squeeze-stile bear half left to join the track which winds down through the bracken and heather moor of Thorngrafton Common. Keep right at the fork, the path now broadened by intensive use by a quadbike. Pass the stone trough en route down to a funnelling entry to a walled lane and gate. The farm track leads to the hamlet of West End Town. The sad ruin of a farm cottage lends a rustic air at the entrance to West End Town Farm. Turn right at the White House through the white gate leading to a galvanised gate and metal kissing-gate beside a barn. Follow the track, breaking left at the wall corner, down the pasture, keeping the burn to the right, as the slope shallows curve with the burn to a (blocked) stile in the corner a few yards right of the gate. Advance with the hedge to the right to a step-stile onto the road. Eschew the seat, keep your pace going! Follow the road right to Westwood Cottages; reaching the road junction go left. When I passed the facing farmyard was staked out in preparation for a housing development. Descend upon the road crossing Chainley Burn, bearing right at the

Low Fogrigg

next junction, ascending the hill to the footpath sign 'Vindolanda 1' right and wall stile. Traverse the pasture half right, left of the pylon. See through the birch-wood the scarred hillside of the old Chainley Colliery. Cross the stile beside the white gate following the green track to an old wooden gate, continuing attractively down an open bank towards Low Fogrigg (cottage). Pass this retreat cottage, probably built by colliers, rising on a pleasant sward track. Notice the curious converging lines of moss covered stones in the adjacent pasture. What did they define? Reach a fixed wicket gate and stile, step over and descend attractively north to a fence stile, shortly fording Doe Sike, continuing via two further fence stiles into the gardens of Chesterholm. Keep assiduously to the path as directed, crossing the Chainley Burn foot-bridge and glancing by the well tended water-gardens. Should you wish to view the remains of Vindolanda with its vicus complex and Wall re-construction it is necessary to obtain a ticket in the museum, a worthwhile investment of time and money. The Vindolanda Trust was founded in 1970 to excavate, preserve and exhibit the extensive Roman military and civilian settlement remains. The fort is in the care of English Heritage. Follow the drive to the grid entrance where turn right ascending a brief portion of Stanegate to the conclusion of the walk.

Roman quarry on Barcombe

Military Way entering Vindolanda's west gate

from ALLEN BANKS ________________________________

6 mile circular walk featuring:
The wooded gorge of the lower Allen and Staward Peel
Shorter options, in no less enchanting surroundings, include
The Tarn in Morralee Wood, and via Briarwood Banks Nature
Reserve and Beltingham - you're spoilt for choice.

The Allen gorge from Staward Peel

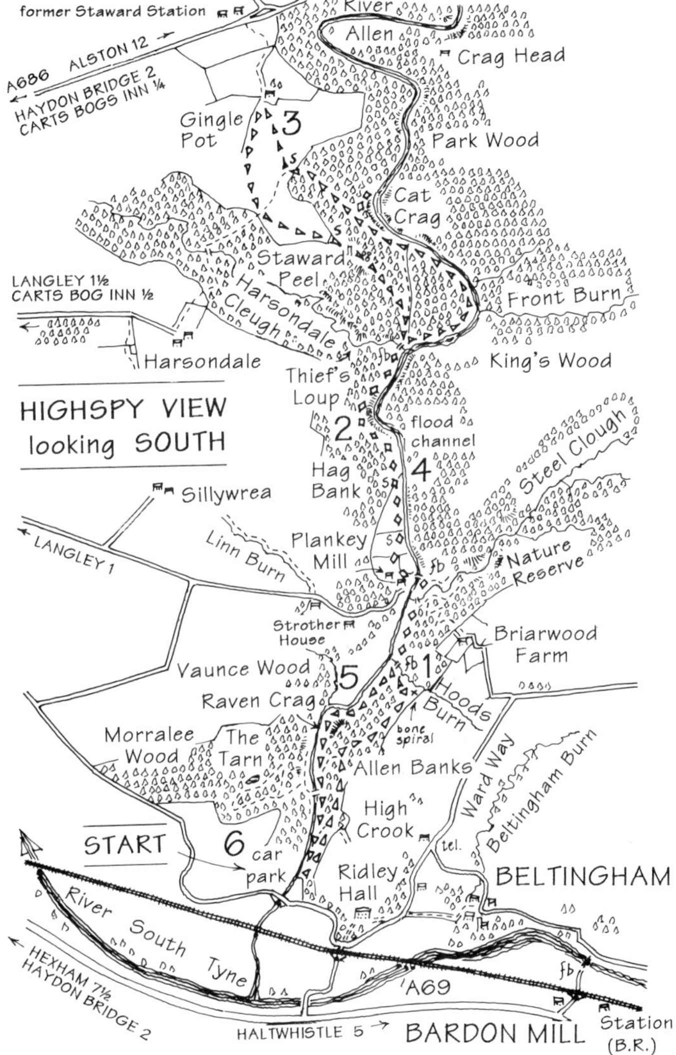

former Staward Station
River Allen
Crag Head
A686 ALSTON 12
HAYDON BRIDGE 2
CARTS BOGS INN ¼
Gingle Pot
3
Park Wood
Cat Crag
LANGLEY 1½
CARTS BOG INN ½
Staward Peel
Harsondale Cleugh
Front Burn
Harsondale
King's Wood
Thief's Loup
HIGHSPY VIEW looking SOUTH
2
flood channel
Steel Clough
Hag Bank
4
Sillywrea
Plankey Mill
Nature Reserve
LANGLEY 1
Linn Burn
fb
Strother House
Briarwood Farm
Vaunce Wood
5
1
Raven Crag
Hoods Burn
bone spiral
Morralee Wood
The Tarn
Allen Banks
Ward Way
Beltingham Burn
START
6
car park
High Crook
Ridley Hall
tel.
BELTINGHAM
River South Tyne
HEXHAM 7½
HAYDON BRIDGE 2
A69
HALTWHISTLE 5
BARDON MILL
Station (B.R.)
fb

| START grid ref. NY 798640 |

Park at the National Trust Allen Banks car park situated three-quarters of a mile from the A69 one mile east of Bardon Mill.   Alternatively, the walk may be accomplished using the regular BR service between Carlisle and Newcastle which stops at Bardon Mill Station. Cross the sturdy footbridge spanning the South Tyne beyond the level crossing and camp site below Mill House Farm.   Follow the minor road east to Beltingham, pronounced 'Beltin-jam'.   This scrupulously neat hamlet has close associations with the Bowes-Lyon family.

Footbridge to Morralee Wood

St. Cuthbert's church, sheltered by a seven hundred year old yew, has a portion of the churchyard devoted to the branch of Bowes-Lyon formerly resident at Ridley Hall (now used as student lodgings for the technical college at Haydon Bridge). A path leads through the dell and on to the road below Ridley Hall: the car park at Allen Banks is only ¼ mile away.

Setting out from the end of Ridley Hall's old walled garden, either branch immediately right, on a gradual ascent by the upper edge of the gorge woodland, or follow the riverside path for a couple of hundred yards, till a flight of stone steps offer a measured ascent right. The elevated path along the lip of the gorge is a delightful parade through the beech fringe, with frequent glimpses across the valley to the densely wooded slopes of Morralee Wood. Graded paths were made on both flanks of the gorge for the exclusive delight of the Bowes-Lyons, who commendably bequeathed these lands to the National Trust.

Approaching the Hoods Burn re-entrant glance right, peer behind a rhododendron bush to find the base of a summer-house, curiously composed of sheep knuckle bones arranged in a spiral, a quirkish device! A zig zagging path descends to the main valley path. Go right, crossing the simple stake bridge, then along the broader path beneath the line of scots pines. In June the clearing at the end is carpeted with wild pansies. Passing the mill ruins the path reaches Kingswood Burn before forking right, immediately prior to the footbridge.

The bridge serves as access to the BRIARWOOD BANKS Nature Reserve: information panel at hand. Here a footpath mounts the ridge to Briarwood Farm from where a return to Beltingham may be made via the farm lane and the Ward Way road.

The Allen at Plankey Mill

However, our journey up this peat stained Orinoco is far from complete. After crossing the footbridge and mounting the rocky knoll the footpath negotiates a suspension bridge to reach Plankey Mill Farm.

Cross the stile directly from the bridge and follow the riverbank upstream to a stile out of the caravan/camping field. The tapering meadows fortuitously starved of modern granular fertiliser and chemical treatment remain a herb-rich treasure trove. Near the end of the meadow, cross the stile left entering the forest, signed 'Pele Tower'. The path has been broadened through the conifers to permit

The Allen flowing over fissured bedrock

easy progress. Another path, tight to the riverbank, gives fine views, however, the way is restricted and leaves the river at a boulder filled flood channel. The log-jam choking its entrance indicates the periodic ferocity of the Allen as it twists and races through a narrow rock shoot, descending again to the little footbridge spanning Harsondale Burn, a secretive pathless ravine entering from the east. Swing right to the site of a footbridge. Crumpled metal supports face each other to confirm the course of an unfordable footpath. Although the valley path goes left beside the broken wall, a more attractive alternative follows the river-bank path, right, affording pleasing views of the Kingswood meadows grazed by cattle. King's Wood and the contiguous Park and Stawardpeel Woods are a recent National Trust acquisition, thus extending the Trust's custodianship of the gorge through from Allen Banks to the A686 at Cupola Bridge. Rejoining the wall-side path through the stone gateway the path ascends and undulates to an unwaymarked fork.

It is well worth considering the brief detour along the righthand path to inspect the dramatic rock slab with an open view of the river. Backtrack to continue upon the ascending shelf path to emerge from the woods at a stile. Footpaths go right and left, ascending the pasture to the skyline. The new footpath, right, leads to the ruined farmstead of Gingle Pot, a superb viewpoint over the wooded Allen gorge particularly north to the Hadrian's Wall horizon from Winshields Crags through Steel Rigg to Rapishaw Gap; neither Vindolanda nor Vercovicium can be seen from this stance.

Dramatic northerly prospect to the Wall, over the wooded Allen gorge from the old Staward station

Should the prospect of mid-walk refreshment appeal then continue along the footpath via three gates to rise onto the Hexham/Alston A686 road, at the former Staward Station: turn left and after three-quarters of a mile of road walking Carts Bog Inn is reached.

From Gingle Pot, follow the wall continuing upon the clear path to the stile giving entry into Harsondale Cleugh. However, ignore this, instead bear left guided by the yellow waymark, to enter the woods at a stile. The path runs upon the crest of a narrowing rock ridge, where heather and bilberry flourish among the oak and birchwood. Shortly a rocky bluff permits breathtaking views into the Allen gorge both north and south. Beyond, the twenty foot high corner remnant of the Staward Peel gatehouse is passed. When in use it composed of a draw-bridge, metal gate and portcullis. On the western brink of the ridge stands a twelve course buttress of dressed sand-stone, the base of the mighty peel erected by the Swin-burnes of Corbridge in the fourteenth century, falling from use three centuries later.

The path makes an abrupt descent to join the valley path beside the wall, where go right to the Harsondale Burn footbridge. Return via Plankey Mill and once across the sus-pension bridge stay upon the valley path which leads below Raven Crag to end the walk downstream.

Coursed masonry of Staward Peel

from ONCE BREWED ________________________________

3 mile circular walk featuring:
The highest point on the Whin Sill scarp

Once Brewed Information Centre and Youth Hostel

START grid ref. NY 753668   Leave the Centre car park turning left and left again (west) along the B6318: an unfortunate beginning with the hazard of speeding traffic. Remember to walk on the right, facing the oncoming traffic. Take great care.

Twice Brewed Inn frequently provokes enquiries as to the origin of its name. There was a time when three hostelries namely East, West and Twice Brewed, served the highway in this isolated locality. The tale dates from Twice Brewed's days as a brew house when its weak beer needed repeated brewing to give it the necessary inebriating effect!

From Highshield Farm to Twice Brewed, the vallum partially coincides with the main road, it then drifts north as a pronounced ditch and double bank through Vallum Lodge Hotel. After what must seem an eternity (½ mile to be precise) Winshields Farm comes into view among mature trees on the right. The footpath sign directs along the access track from the entrance gate. Pass through the farmyard, as directed, left via gates. The subsequent track crosses the damaged Vallum on course for the rising dip slope of Winshields Crag. Passing rejected farm machinery, the track mounts more steeply, diverts from the track half left to ascend the slope. Enter Lodhams Slack via a fence. The name is contradictory, for lodhams describes a 'muddy place', and slack means 'dry stony valley'. The cattle and sheep that graze these pastures do their level best to keep the soil well poached (muddy). On gaining the ridge wall in a shallow depression, go right to the summit of Winshields Crag. At 1132 feet this is the highest point on

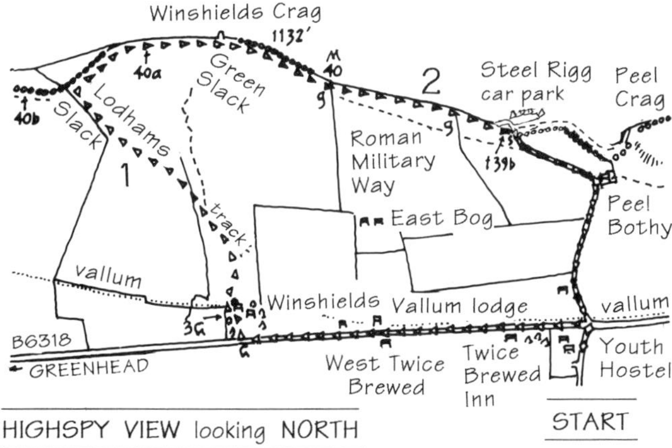

HIGHSPY VIEW looking NORTH   START

the Whin Sill, the culminating point marked by a now redundant Ordnance Survey triangulation column. For many years a telescope gave visitors a better view, but this has recently been uprooted and dragged down the slope. Naturally this is a panoramic viewpoint, but few features command special eminence (hence the merit of the telescope): the Whin Sill from the Nine Nicks of Thirlwall to Sewingshields Crag with the dark mass of the Wark Forest filling the northern skyline, with its military mast prominent; the southern horizon is filled by the broad expanse of Pennine Fells drained by the rivers Allen and South Tyne.

Prospect east on the descent from Winshields Crag

Commence the descent admiring the wall upon the Wall foundation which has an interesting mosaic pattern in the vicinity of Milecastle 40. The Pathfinder map persists in depicting the footpath (impossibly) on the north side of the wall during this descent. Pass through two wicket-gates, cross the ladder stile, and the road. The enticement of walking beside the Clayton Wall will doubtless prove too much to resist. Follow this splendid section enjoying the wonderful prospect of the Whin Sill scarp ahead. Curving with the Wall down to a ladder-stile right, above Peel Gap, join the road via a ladder-stile directly above Peel Bothy, a Landmark Trust property. Turn downhill to the National Park Centre car park.

from CAWFIELDS ____

2¼ mile circular walk featuring:
Caw Gap, Thorny Doors and Milecastle 42

Cawfield Crags

START grid ref. NY 712666

From the Northumberland National Park Cawfields Picnic Site car park pass the flooded whinstone quarry advancing to the kissing-gate approaching Hole Gap. Go left onto the Cawfields Farm drive. Pass the farm via gates continuing as if to East Cawfields branching right off the track to a field gate. Cross the ensuing pasture to a narrow gate, keeping the wall to the left-hand side. Via a gate to the minor road, go right. The gradient increases to Caw Gap beyond the junction with the Steel Rigg road. Turn right through the wicket-gate: you are now upon the WALL WALK.

Rise with low consolidated Wall at your feet. Pass the outline of turret 41a crossing the crest via a stile before descending the stepped path to Thorny Doors. Progressing along the scarp beside the substantial Wall enjoy the views over the edge to Cawfields. The ridge dips gently down to Milecastle 42 which is rather oddly perched at an awkward angle above Hole Gap.

For a good view back upon the milecastle climb to the crest of the quarry severed peak, before passing through the kissing-gate to return.

STANEGATE OPTION

As a variation you might opt to ascend Cawfield Crags direct to Thorny Doors and Caw Gap then either backtrack, or return gently via the Roman Military Way.

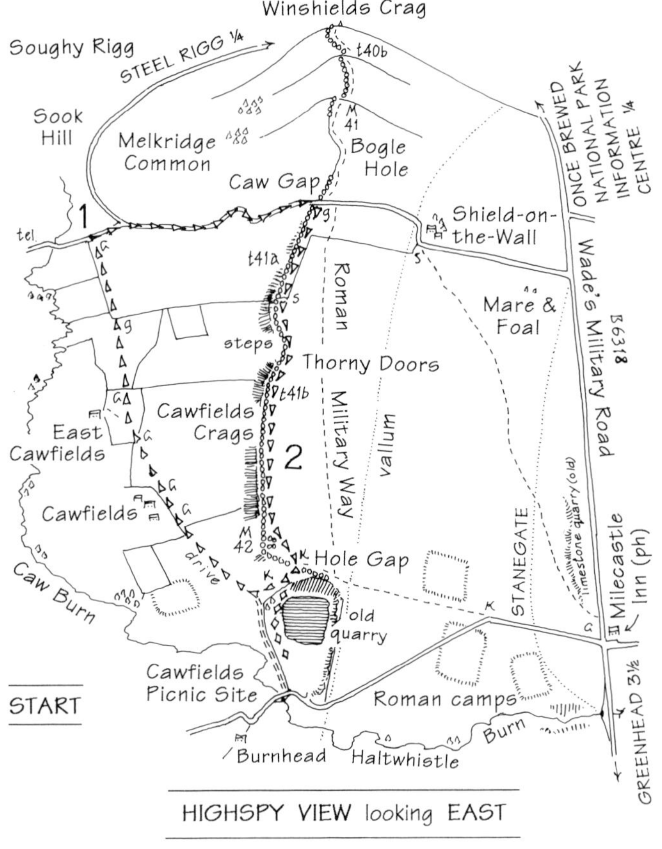

HIGHSPY VIEW looking EAST

Better still follow the road from Caw Gap to Shield-in-the-Wall diverting right at a stile at the second bend to make the long traverse of the open pasture to the Milecastle Inn. This allows you to view the handsome length of vallum and then to accompany a notable stretch of Stanegate, well marked underfoot as a turf causeway: the road leading north gives a view over the Haltwhistle Burn Stanegate fort.

To return to Hole Gap keep straight ahead at the left-hand bend through the gate. Note the traces of two temporary encampments probably associated with the legionaries who built the Wall.

The Wall rising east along the crest of Cawfield Crags

Looking west over Caw Gap from Bogle Hole

Mare and Foal standing stones

Looking east along Stanegate littered with mole-hills,
notice the 'Mare and Foal' on the horizon

from HALTWHISTLE ______________________________ _____

5 mile circular walk featuring:
Haltwhistle Burn, Great Chesters and Milecastle 42

Cawfields Crags from Burnhead

START grid ref. NY 713642

The path up the Haltwhistle Burn to the Military Road is a popular local stroll. Formerly disfigured by coal mining this delightful secluded gorge has to all intents been reclaimed by nature.

Beginning from Town Foot Bridge, follow the track leading upstream from the west side of the bridge. Passing tree plantings on the old mine rail embankment, a path continues beside the burn, at this point known to local lads as 'Spooky Forest'. Eschewing steps onto the recreation ground and the inviting white railed footbridge, advance upstream to join the minor road. Beyond the old brick glazing works leave the road, cross the access bridge and follow the path through

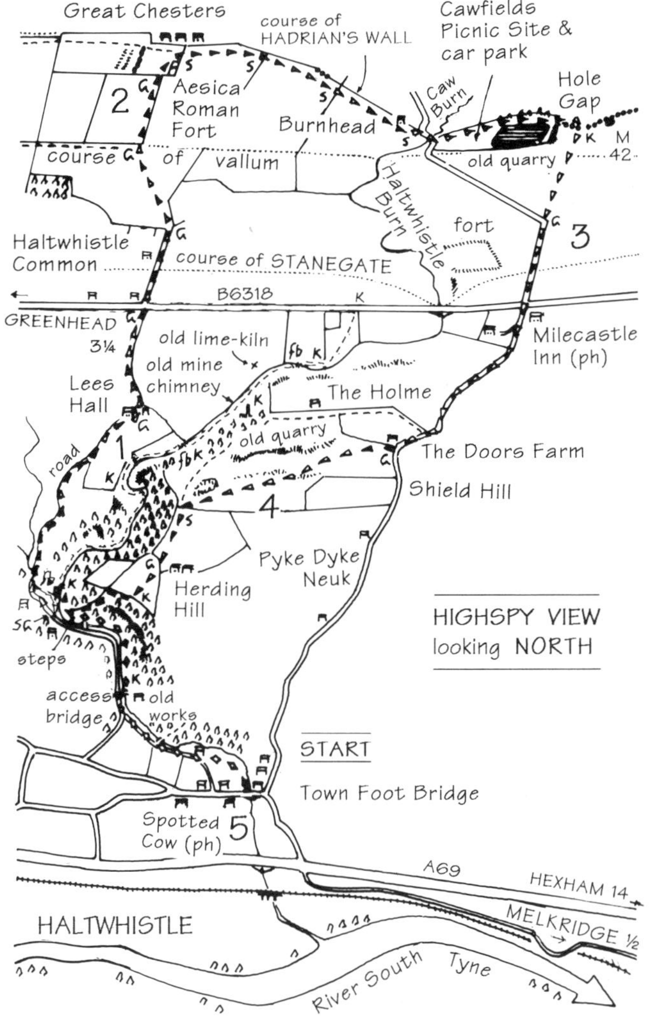

Great Chesters
course of HADRIAN'S WALL
Cawfields Picnic Site & car park
Caw Burn
Hole Gap
Aesica Roman Fort
Burnhead
2
course of vallum
Haltwhistle Burn
old quarry
K M 42
fort
3
Haltwhistle Common
course of STANEGATE
B6318
K
GREENHEAD 3¼
old lime-kiln
old mine chimney
fb k
The Holme
Milecastle Inn (ph)
Lees Hall
road
1
K
fb k
old quarry
The Doors Farm
Shield Hill
4
HIGHSPY VIEW looking NORTH
Pyke Dyke Neuk
Herding Hill
K
steps
access bridge
old works
START
Town Foot Bridge
Spotted Cow (ph)
5
A69
HEXHAM 14
MELKRIDGE ½
HALTWHISTLE
River South Tyne

the kissing-gate: now on the east bank leading past old quarry workings and the discreet entrance to a drift coal mine. Notice the steps to Doors Farm rising right, called Cat Stairs, probably alluding to the polecat. These feature on the return leg of the walk.

The valley path advances to cross the footbridge/gate. At this point it is necessary to bear left to a stile/gate onto the road. The locally popular valley path continuing from the footbridge initially runs upstream on the west bank of Haltwhistle Burn via kissing-gates, later crossing a third footbridge before rising onto the Military Road. Though scenically satisfying, this fine path has no legal status. It passes beneath another old quarry and through a wild craggy curving gorge, to pass a tall chimney, the second in the valley. This remnant of an engine house marks the site of a long abandoned drift mine. Like many similar ventures mining ceased because of excessive flooding. Across the stream under the ridge and furrow in the pasture bank stands a triple arched lime-kiln: evidence of agricultural activities in recent centuries, more especially during the last century when greater acreages were put under the plough. Regular dressings of burnt lime combated the natural acidity of the soil enabling farmers to produce useful crops of corn and vigorous grass sward. Now much of the area has reverted to acidity as few tenants can contemplate the cost of such applications. Lime today comes from Prudhoe.

Ascend the road leading up by Broomhaw Hall via a gate to pass round to the right of Lee Hall Farm. Continue along the access track to a gate onto the Military Road. Go right then left at the cottage. The lane leads down by Markham Cottage to a gate. An unenclosed track advances towards Great Chesters Farm, clearly in view across the valley. Crossing the vallum rise up to the Roman Fort of Aesica via two gates. Note the masonry belonging to the periphery of the fort degenerated to rubbing posts of dairy cattle! In the centre of the close see the fenced off sunken strong- room.

Guardhouse in the south-west corner of Aesica

Cawfields Quarry

Go right to leave the fort over a ladder-stile in the company of the Pennine Way. Heading eastward the footpath crosses stiles as it runs beside the Roman Wall.

Note the eighteenth century field boundary, with many Roman stones crudely used. Ancient wall foundations are detectable where the wall kinks in the second field. Cross the stile just below Burnhead Cottage, newly enlarged and renovated, thus joining the road. Cross Haltwhistle Burn, go left and right to enter the National Park Cawfield Crags picnic site car park. Follow the fenced path along the north bank of the quarry lake. Focus attention upon the impressive volcanic peak created by early twentieth century quarrying. However did the quarrymen gain licence to do this devastation to dear old Hadrian's Wall? At Hole Gap pass through the kissing-gate; make a point of inspecting Milecastle 42 awkwardly perched on a slope. A short spur climb right in a fenced path reaches a crest where the quarry has severed the wall. Survey the dark waters and the milecastle from on high.

Return to the Hole Gap depression. Follow the bridlepath leading south from the pass, once more crossing the vallum and glancing by a Roman marching camp, associated with the earlier Stanegate system. Pass through the gate onto the minor road used by the majority of visitors to the Cawfields car park. Continue south, crossing the line of Stanegate, going directly over the Milecastle Inn cross-roads. This rendezvous for

The Milecastle Inn

nourishment can be heartily recommended, the author having partaken of many a fine meal here over recent years!

Continue along the minor road for a further third of a mile. Seek the second signposted footpath right, at a gate, leading diagonally across a low ridge with evidence of long abandoned quarrying. Descend a shallow pasture passing to the left of a fenced quarry with silver birch (note the crude bothy within!), advancing to the edge overlooking the pine and heather fringed Haltwhistle Burn. At this point on my excursion I spotted a flock of jackdaws and pigeons turning tail on a peregrine.

Arriving at a wall stile beside this fine viewpoint proceed down the pasture to a gate below Herding Hill Farm. Maintain a southerly course to the kissing-gate. The confined path goes right past a seat at the wooded brink of the valley: presumably before the valley gained the attention of coal miners this path continued on line into the valley floor. On the latter part of the stepped descent glimpse the cutting running away from the exit of the drift mine, which is tucked in the bank directly below. Upon regaining the valley path either cross the bridge straight ahead, to join the road early, or follow the path downstream used on the outward stage of the walk. Conclude as you began on the path beside Haltwhistle Burn, glancing past the recreation ground to finish at Town Foot.

The Spotted Cow - noted for canny ale, canny food and canny crack!

4½ mile circular walk featuring:
Aesica Roman Fort, Mucklebank Crag and Blake Law

Mucklebank Crag - looking west towards Walltown Crags

START grid ref. NY 712666

From Cawfields National Park picnic site/car park accompany the Pennine Way waymarks west. Cross the Caw Burn road bridge, branching left at the ladder-stile on the line of Hadrian's Wall. On the high banks, flanking the burn downstream, beside Stanegate lie the outlines of two Roman encampments: considered to have formed the bases for legionaries involved in the construction of the Wall. From here to Great Chesters the scarp diminishes. Pass Burnhead Cottage recently renovated, then accompany the field wall built upon the Roman frontier. Occasional Roman stones are apparent though most have been more widely dispersed throughout local field boundaries. The wall bends beyond the next stile. Note evidence of the survival of Wall core about the site of turret 42b. Users of the Pathfinder map will notice an anomaly: the Pennine Way is shown following the Roman Military Way a little to the south of the waymarked route. After the next stile the footpath passes Great Chesters farmhouse and, mounting a shallow bank, reaches a stile to enter Aesica, Great Chesters Roman Fort; its antiquarian interest subservient to the demands of a working dairy farm.

In traversing the paddock note the arch in its midst, the remains of the underground strong-room vault first excavated in 1894. This fort, the tenth along the frontier, extends to three acres and was base for 500 infantrymen of the 2nd Cohort of Asturians. The most remarkable

Strong-room vault in the middle of the fort enclosure

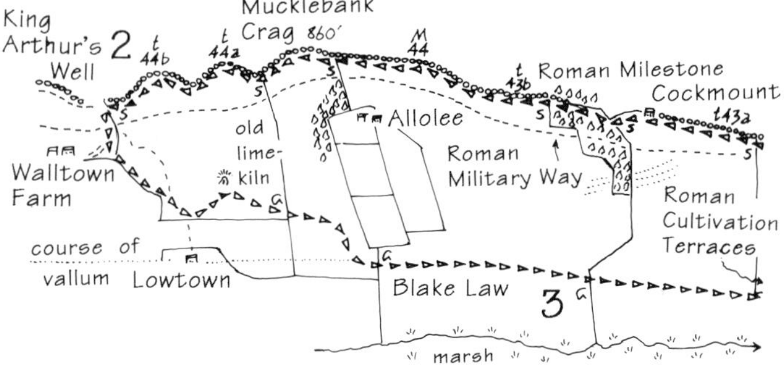

feature of Aesica was its water supply: as the site had insufficient natural springs to service its large population they engineered a leat from Tom Fond's Pool on the Caw Burn which drains Greenlee Lough. In order to maintain a steady fall the aqueduct took a contorted six mile course to reach the fort in the vicinity of the present-day farm. Like Brocolitia, the fort was built in the strengthening phase, around 132 A.D. Milecastle 43 was incorporated below the north wall, mimmicking Vercovicium's rounded corners. The fort has been partially consolidated, though the eastern side has been lost to agricultural enclosure. The whole fort is sited on unenhanced farmland, therefore curious visitors have to contend with nettles and cowpats.

Old lime-kiln above Lowtown

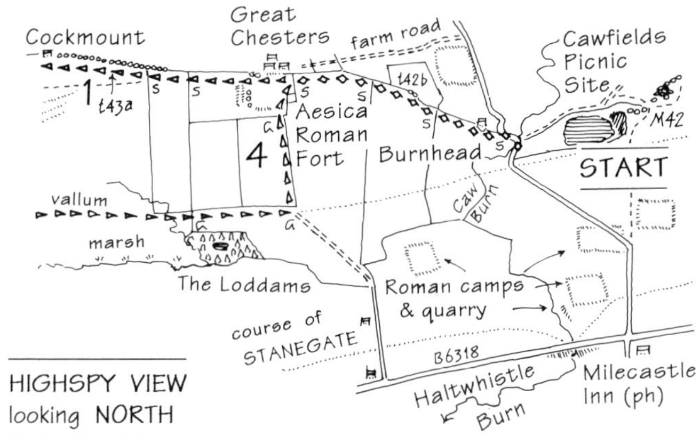

HIGHSPY VIEW
looking NORTH

Leave the fort by its west gate, noting the extra ramparts to this side. Proceed via two stiles and passing Cockmount Hill enter woodland via a ladder-stile. The cultivation terracing down the southern slope may have had Roman origins, though it is more likely to be a manifestation of medieval peasantry.

The woodland, a mix of scots pine and self-seeded willow, is a pleasant contrast to the surrounding open hill pasture. Exit from the plantation over a stile; note the unusual

Cockmount Hill

Mucklebank Crag

gatepost to the right. This Roman Milestone was 'gifted' to an eighteenth century farmer by his Latin predecessors, who deftly lifted it from the adjacent Military Way! The footpath clings to the crude low wall along the line of the Roman Wall. Crossing further stiles enjoy the views from Mucklebank Crag, the highest hill among the Nine Nicks of Thirlwall. On reaching Walltown Gap via a stile, notice King Arthur's Well: legend associates this spot with the baptism of King Edwin of Northumberland. Edwin ruled the Deira division of the kingdom of Northumbria during the early seventh century, was baptised a Christian by Paulinius, the missionary monk, in 627 A.D. It would appear to be a spot steeped in Arthurian legend too, though in what connection is unclear, as he is also linked with the Sewingshields eastern end of the dolerite scarp, hence King's Wicket and King's Hill, near Housesteads.

Turn down left, branch left, rather than passing Walltown Farm. Follow Allolee's access track, pass by the broken lime kiln to a gate, thereafter keep on the right-hand track which leads to a further gate and the low ridge of Blake Law, the natural dry line adopted for the barely recognisable vallum. The marshland gives an interesting natural history contrast. The name Loddams appropriately translates to 'muddy meadow', though walkers are not thus encumbered. The cultivation terraces below Cockmount can be seen more clearly from this level and always ahead rise Cawfield Crags and Winshields Crag, the highest point on the Whin Sill.

Pass through two gates en route to the approach track to Great Chesters Farm. Arriving from the right, this humble way is indubitably Roman, linking the Stanegate with the fort's southern entry. Go left through the gate ascending the slightly sunken track towards the farm. On this flank of the fort lay a small vicus (civil settlement) and covered for safe keeping is a hypocaust chamber. At a gate enter the south gateway of the fort, set, you may notice, with an eastern bias, which may reflect the layout of the principal buildings within the fort. The almost casual array of Roman masonry associated with the excavated southern gateway is a striking

Roman Milestone from the Stanegate functioning as a gatepost

109

reminder of the archaeology lurking beneath this rustic scene. Branch right to the ladder-stile previously crossed to conclude the walk to Cawfields Quarry picnic site.

Turret 44b

Impressive eastern prospect along the Wall from Great Chesters Farm

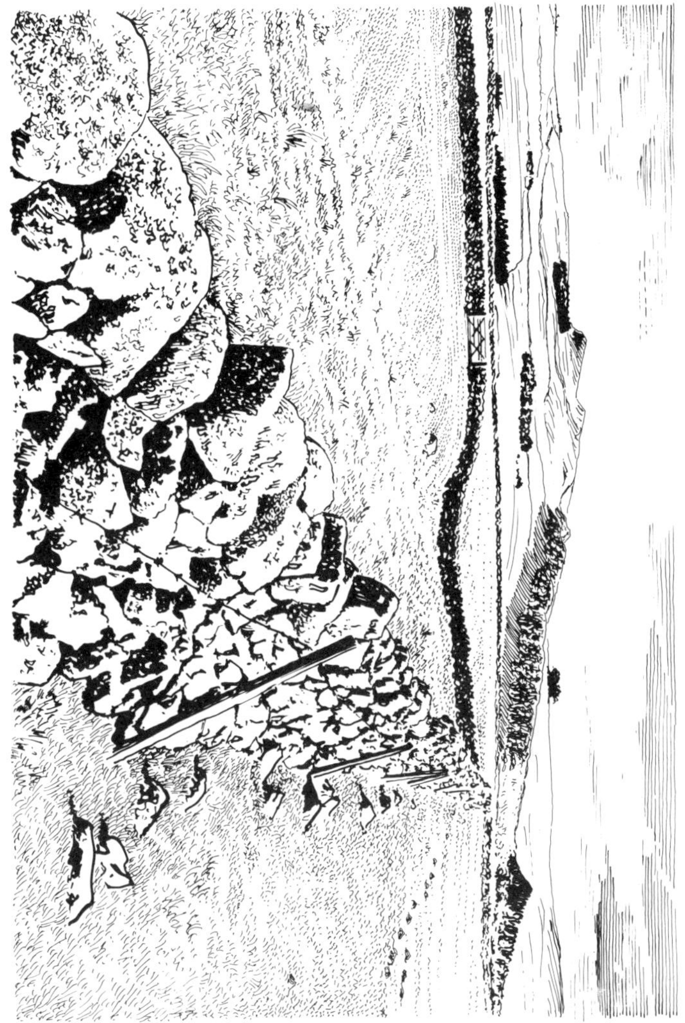

Cawfield and Winshields Crags from Cockmount Hill

3 mile circular walk featuring:
The Roman Wall in grand parade along Walltown Crags

Walltown backed by Cold Fell from turret 44b

START grid ref. NY 675662

Park in the parking space on the unenclosed road to Walltown Farm (which branches right from the minor road a few yards north of the entrance to Carvoran Roman Army Museum). It is the intention of Northumberland National Park to open Walltown Quarry as a picnic site, replacing the small lay-by car park adopted as the start (and finish) of this walk.

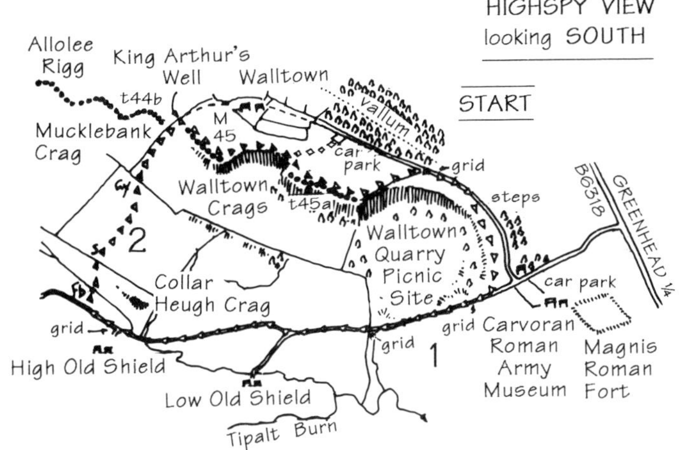

Ascend the slope due north to arrive at the lip of the old Walltown Crags Quarry, with its central pond and, no doubt, a cattle feeding rack in attendance. Bear left passing turret 45a taking close company with the unusually switchback course of the Wall, an intriguing passage terminated cruelly by the whinstone quarry, now landscaped. Follow the quarry-edge wall down to the cattle grid and along the road right. An adjacent path relieves pedestrians from unwelcome encounters with cars begun at steps. This leads round to the cattle grid (where the Pennine Way departs west). Continue north upon the unenclosed road via two further cattle grids, and 250 yards beyond the entrance to High Old Shield strike right crossing a plank footbridge, climbing the bank to a ladder-stile in the wall running along the top of the Collar Heugh sub-scarp. Cross the cattle pasture half left to a gateway. Complete the ascent into the natural breach of the Whin Sill scarp, making the depression where issues King Arthur's Well. Either follow the open track and succeeding road down through the shrunken 'township of Walltown' to the car park, or, preferably, climb beside the Wall's core pillow bank up to the scarp edge (this path carries no right-of-way) again progressing attractively west. But just as the Wall grows several courses the quarry intervenes, forcing the path left beside a fence. The quarry edge and sheer face is poorly protected here, so do keep 'young charges' behind the fence. The view east to Mucklebank and beyond to Winshields Crag is notable. Drift away from the edge of the quarry to descend to the car park.

Wall culvert looking to Low Old Shield

Exciting switchback course of the Roman Wall on Walltown Crags

Walltown Quarry looking to Mucklebank Crag from the vicinity
of turret 45a, at the site of a Stanegate Beacon (signal station)

from GREENHEAD ________________________________

2 mile circular walk featuring: Magnis Roman Fort,
Carvoran Roman Army Museum and Thirlwall Castle

Cross Fell from the north-west corner of Magnis Roman Fort

START grid ref. NY 660654

Park in Station Road near Greenhead Youth Hostel.
Follow the B6318 east crossing the Tipalt Bridge to
pass Glenwhelt House formerly known as The Globe in the
days when it was a coaching inn. Admire the cobbles and the
classical doorway crowned by a flaming sun plaque bearing
the date 1757. Glenwhelt pre-dates Greenhead, the community long connected with the Blenkinsopp estate. The
arrival of the Newcastle to Carlisle Railway finished the
coaching trade, but the exploitation of seams of coal and
limestone for agricultural improvement within the immediate
locality created Greenhead at the expense of Glenwhelt.

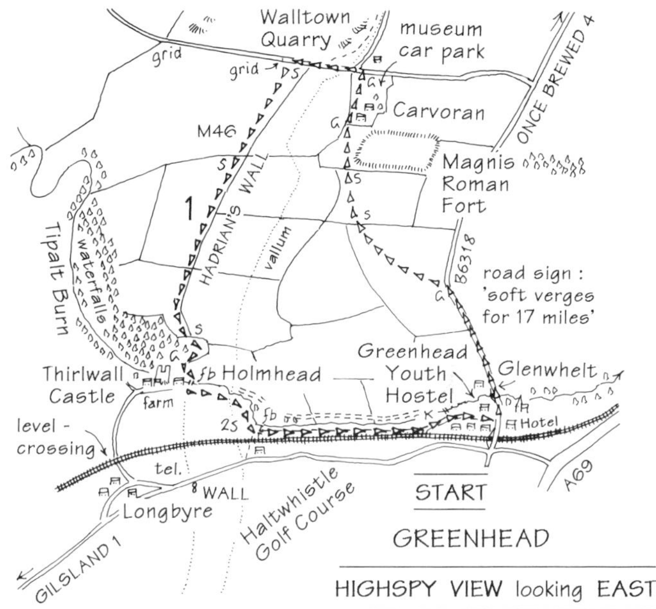

At the top of the steep initial gradient, where the road bends, go left through the gate traversing the arable field half right to a stile. Continue crossing the invisible course of Stanegate to a second stile over the wall bounding Magnis Roman Fort. As the opening drawing to this description shows even if the fort lacks visible excitement the view through the upper South Tyne valley corridor to Cross Fell, at 2930 ft/893 metres the highest ground on the Pennine chain, is a special feature. Your eyes may trace the course of Maiden Way, which crosses the high Pennine divide above Alston.

Pass on to the gate beside the former Carvoran Farm, owned and imaginatively developed by Robin Burley, director of the Vindolanda Trust, and dedicated to the exhibition of life on the Wall for the Roman soldier. The Roman Army Museum (entry fee) is an experience to be recommended (shop/cafe).

Carvoran

Proceed through the museum visitors car park to the road. Go left, linking with the Pennine Way by the landscaped Walltown Quarry, following the road north. Just short of the cattle-grid divert left over the stile to follow the north ditch and eighteenth century enclosure wall.

Walltown Quarry

The rather uneventful outline of Magnis Roman Fort is in view to the left, thought to have been built contemporaneously with Stanegate, situated at its junction with the Maiden Way. However, no trace of pre-Hadrianic timber structure has been found. At 3½ acres this was the smallest fort along the Wall's length, and awaits systematic excavation. The vallum makes a regular angled kink north of the fort, probably simply to negotiate boggy ground. The **Pennine Way** crosses a ladder-stile after the enigmatic site of Milecastle 46, from where there is a splendid view west over the drumlin landscape towards Gilsland. The north ditch features prominently, stretching beyond Haltwhistle golf course to the Irthing gorge. This intervening country forms the main Pennine watershed. Prior to the Ice Age the Irthing made union with the Tyne, a glacial moraine dam (drumlins) forcing the river to cut a westerly course to join the Eden. Although the mid-eighteenth century Military Road (A69) took the obvious course from Greenhead, south of the Irthing to Brampton, the Romans appear to have been influenced by their existing Pike Hill Signal Station and made a stategic strike for the higher ground leading to it; unlike Stanegate which ran across the slopes south of the river.

Pennine Way and Wall Walk footbridge over the Tipalt at Holmhead

The two false pillars set into the low barn at Holmhead mark the course of Hadrian's Wall and were inserted at the behest of John Clayton

At the foot of the bank cross a ladder-stile and wind down to a gate at Holmhead. Crossing the Tipalt foot-bridge gaze up to the romantic ruins of Thirlwall Castle (no access), built in the turbulent twelfth century, from Roman Wall and Carvoran masonry. It is strategically placed, at the end of the Whin Sill scarp, effecting control on access to and from the wild north country of Border Reiver infamy. On 20 September 1306 Edward I stayed here during his ill-fated campaign against the Scots (a memorial erected by the Duke of Norfolk stands on the marshes near Burgh-by-Sands). Thirlwall Castle fell from grace after four hundred years of iron hand, the hanging walls today tantalisingly teetering over the Tipalt.

Beyond the Duffenfoot cottages turn left following the burnside path to Pow Charney Beck. Eschew crossing the Newcastle to Carlisle inter-city railway. Instead, cross the Pow Charney foot-bridge progressing left along the confined passage between the Tipalt and the railway to re-enter Station Road.

Thirlwall Castle simply laden
with Roman masonry

Greenhead
Youth Hostel

FEATHERSTONE CASTLE 18

from HALTWHISTLE

A 9 mile circular walk featuring:
Bellister Castle, Iron Age settlement on Broomhouse
Common, Park Burn Falls, South Tyne Railway, Lambley
Viaduct, Featherstone Castle and Wydon Nabb

Bellister Castle

Haltwhistle lies not only at the Heart of Wall Country,
but, far more significantly, at the 'Centre of Britain'.

START grid ref. NY 703642

On driving into Haltwhistle
follow the brown signs for
the Tourist Information Office, situated adjacent to the
swimming pool. Walk from the capacious car park
retracing your approach down Greenholme Road council
estate. Turn left into Greencroft Avenue and proceed to
the main street next to a useful Tourist Information
town map stand and phone-card kiosk. Cross over,
continue past the Railway Hotel and negotiate the
pedestrian crossing: there are plans to create a by-
pass to ameliorate the effect of the A69 through
this constricted western end of Haltwhistle. Go left,
then right, passing under the railway to cross the broad

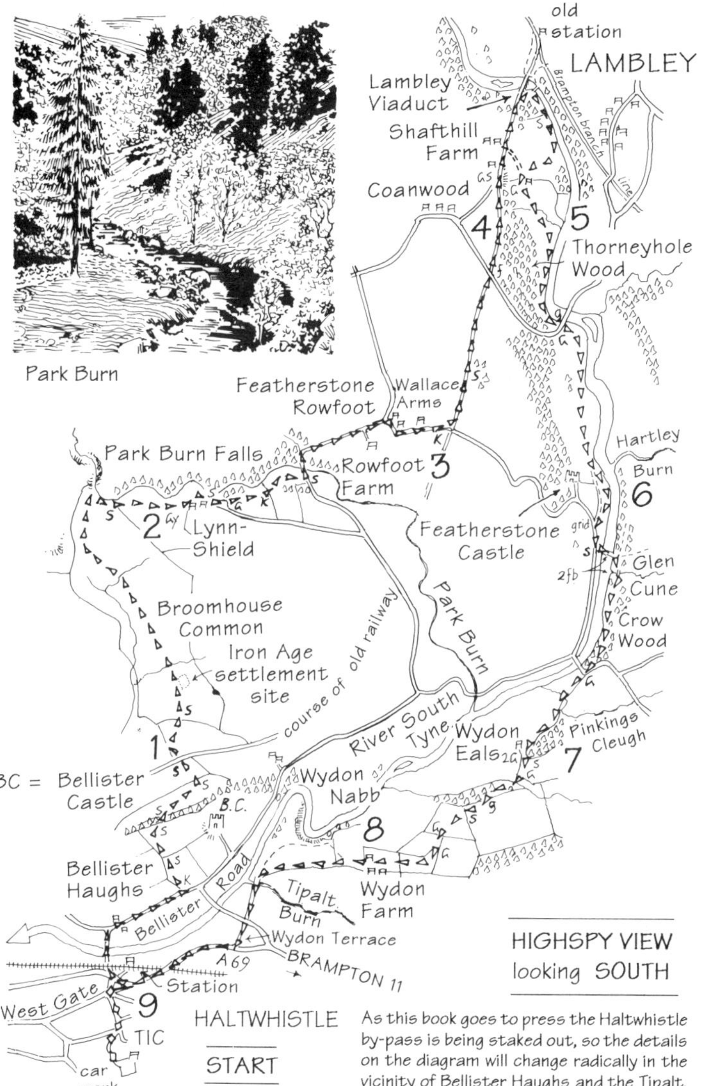

As this book goes to press the Haltwhistle by-pass is being staked out, so the details on the diagram will change radically in the vicinity of Bellister Haughs and the Tipalt.

West Gate,
Haltwhistle

South Tyne via the pedestrian bridge (built as a road bridge in 1875): down river is the old Alston branch line railway bridge, known as Alston Arches. On reaching the minor road turn right. Notice the house with protruding tie blocks, obviously originally intended for a semi-detached pairing; this quirky device occurs elsewhere in Haltwhistle. Follow Bellister Road for 450 yards to an 'elderly' kissing-gate left, where the footpath sign indicates 'Broomhouse Common 1'. Keeping the hedge to the left proceed on a southerly course across Bellister Haugh. Pass the stock-watering hollow, exploiting a subterranean stream. Crossing the stile notice the winding hollow running sympathetic with the footpath; this was the old river-bed of the South Tyne.

The river formerly ran to the south of Bellister Castle, which can be seen perched upon a motte over to the right. Quite the most charming little castle, a night under its roof is a memorable experience. Beautifully restored, Bellister belongs to the National Trust. Its creaking timberwork and hoary stone walls harbour the spirit of a wandering minstrel, who called one night seeking lodgings. Not content to simply turn him away, the master of the house set his hounds on the poor wretch. The cruel murder that ensued haunts the environs to this day!

Advance to the fence-stile, ascend the scrubby woodland bank to the fence-stile at the top. Bearing half right, rise across the pasture bank, cross the step stile over the rigg-top wall. Descend straight to a stile thereby crossing the old railway trackbed. Angle round the marshy hollow, heavily 'poached' by cattle, via a plank bridge to ascend the facing hillside. Crossing a wall ladder-stile enter moorland bedecked with bracken and boulders. Continue almost due south, within 250 yards encountering the perimeter ditch of an Iron Age settlement. The rectangle measures 60 x 40 of the author's modest paces. Two hut circles 11 paces wide and a linear wall feature can be identified within. Broomhouse Common,

Park Burn Falls

the haunt of golden plover and red grouse, provides an especially delightful interlude. Keeping west of the main stream head south, cross two side streams before bearing right short of an intervening enclosure wall. Follow a low ridge to a picturesque amphitheatre overlooking Park Burn, a prime spot to sit; take a break and admire the central waterfall feature below.

Go right, downstream, to a ladder-stile. Enjoy the wooded confines of Park Burn whilst advancing to a gateway leading down beside Lynnshield, which means 'summer shelter by the waterfalls'. Cross the stile to join the farm road. Branch right at the first gate (no waymark), descend the pasture in sympathy with Park Burn. After the kissing-gate angle left down the valley bank traversing the meadow to a stile onto the road. Go left ascending the hill, advancing to the Featherstone Rowfoot junction. Go right perhaps allowing yourself a chance to sample something from the 'Hexhamshire Brewery' served up at the Wallace Arms Hotel, known to locals as 'The South Jerry' (the 'North Jerry' being The Milecastle Inn, on the Military Road). Descending the road from the pub, access the rail track-bed by branching half left through an allied car park and kissing-gate. Follow the trackbed south, part of the South Tyne Trail, via an intervening stile to a picnic site. Cross the road, negotiating the paling fence and continue on the line of the railway, initially confined by broom. Pass a seat from where one can enjoy the fine westerly views over the South Tyne. Notice the sturdy buffer, one of few items of railway furniture to survive the demise of the line, as too the hand water-pump (right) encountered after the cottage (depository of classic cars). Cross the stile left of the gate to continue along the trackbed south towards Lambley Viaduct. Cross a stile, subsequently

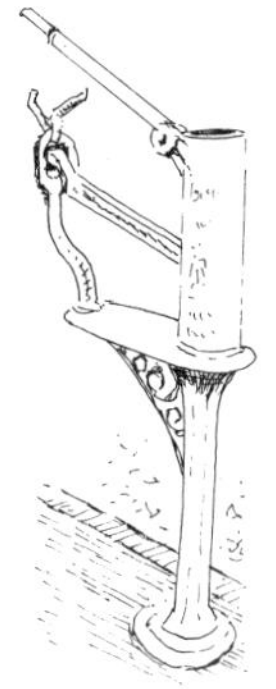

Lambley Viaduct from the banks of the South Tyne

slipping through an intervening light fence to reach the threshold of the viaduct.   Marvel at the South Tyne sweeping grandly below, a scene once prized by railway travellers. Either backtrack to Shafthill Farm, descending the bank in a north-westerly direction to a gate by the renovated cottage, or make the steep descent directly from the viaduct on its west side which leads to a riverside path.   Until 1992 a footbridge clung to the viaduct piers. Crumbling masonry required the erection of a new structure a safe distance downstream.   Do not cross,

Featherstone Castle

instead follow the footpath downstream crossing a stile keeping to the floodbank for 250 yards before bearing right to reach the gate, mentioned previously for easy descent from the trackbed. Pass the renovated cottage. Advance north, no discernible path underfoot, to accompany the river beneath Thorneyhole Wood to hand-gate on to the A689. Bear slightly right in crossing the highway to a wicket-gate. Entering Featherstone Park follow the unenclosed track, via a gate, passing the remnants of a prisoner-of-war camp and defunct sewage works. After the camp the track becomes a roadway, glancing past Featherstone Castle. Featherstone Castle is a private home; should you wish to gain a closer look at this intriguing fortified mansion heed the need to respect the owner's privacy. Photographically it makes a fine subject with parkland trees and cattle grazing the Tyne meadows - though wretched BSE may influence the presence of the latter!

Pass a weir to join the minor road at a cattle-grid. After just fifty yards cross the stile left (footpath sign 'Wydon Eals 1') and the footbridge over the South Tyne. Ignore the inviting rising steps; instead go right. Cross Glencune Burn footbridge, continue through pines beside the Tyne on an undulating and frequently narrow path through Crow Wood to join the minor road. Branch immediately left down the drive signed 'Wydon Eals ½, Haltwhistle 2½'. Waymarks guide left of the farm via two gates and a stile. Branch from the track with

Wydon Nabb

Cold Fell from Wydon Nabb

waymarks directing down to a galvanised gate. Ford the burn. Ascend the bank in a shallow hollow-way rise 170 yards to a wicket-gate at the top of the wooded bank (waymarking a bit vague from the ford). Entering pastureland follow the fence right to a stile, then aim for the right of the two gates across the next field. Descend to a gate onto a farm track, pass through Wydon farmyard and along the farm drive. The drive passes beneath the northern dip slope of Wydon Nabb, a scar exposure of Whin Sill dyke. Though not a right-of-way walkers may be tempted to view this little suspected grand sweep of the South Tyne backed by Cold Fell. This can be easily achieved by branching from the road 200 yards after the farm, rising over the pasture via an old hedge-line to the fenced brink, returning to the road in a natural sweep past the life-belt! THE IMMINENT A69 BY-PASS WILL AFFECT THE ROUTE HEREON SHORTLY. Cross a cattle-grid and Tipalt Burn bridge, ascending into Haltwhistle, then cross the road into Wydon Terrace continuing onto the narrow pavement into the town.

CENTRE of BRITAIN WALK 19
from   BARDON MILL STATION

A 5½ mile linear walk to Haltwhistle allow 2½ hours
featuring: Willimonteswick, Unthank Hall, Plenmeller
and the Centre of Britain

Logo of CENTRE OF BRITAIN LTD - by kind permission

START grid ref. NY779646

A car-free walk to the Centre of Britain. Now doesn't that tantalise the imagination? The regularity and convenience of trains and buses running through the Tyne Gap between Carlisle and Newcastle make it so easy to plan a walk on the spur of the moment, at any season of the year. Add to this facility sure refreshment at either end, gentle terrain, quiet country ways and a unique 'centralist' objective, and a couple of healthy hours' good walking must ensue. If you arrive by

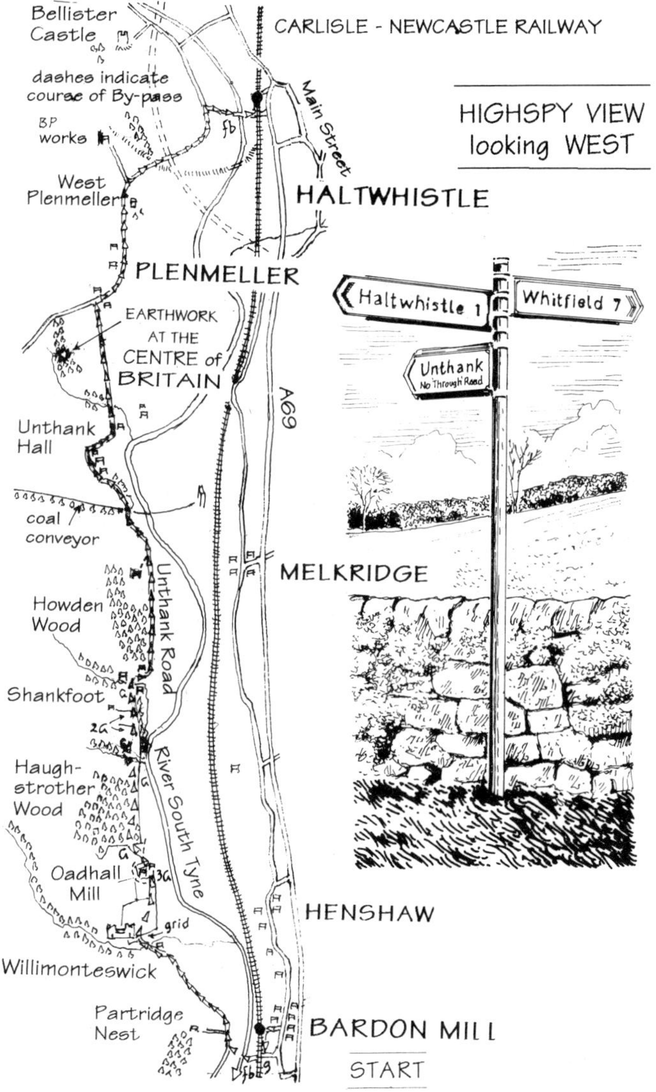
Bellister Castle
dashes indicate course of By-pass
BP works
West Plenmeller
CARLISLE - NEWCASTLE RAILWAY
Main Street
HALTWHISTLE
fb
PLENMELLER
EARTHWORK AT THE CENTRE of BRITAIN
Unthank Hall
coal conveyor
A69
Unthank Road
Howden Wood
Shankfoot
2G
Haugh-strother Wood
River South Tyne
Oadhall Mill
3G
grid
Willimonteswick
Partridge Nest
fb
BARDON MILL
HENSHAW
MELKRIDGE
HIGHSPY VIEW looking WEST
Haltwhistle 1
Whitfield 7
Unthank
No Through Road
START

Errington Reay Pottery

car park in Haltwhistle and take one of the hourly buses or trains to Bardon Mill, the next halt east. With canny planning you might (as the author and his wife one February weekday) sneak into the Bowes Arms for a light lunch before setting forth. The name derives from the Bowes-Lyon family formerly of Ridley Hall across the river at Beltingham (pronounced 'Bel-tinge-ham'); you may recognise the connection with H.R.H. the Queen Mother, who was also a Bowes-Lyon. There is modest car parking space in the village centre opposite the pub and village stores, but this is strictly for residents. Before heading off take a glance at the adjacent Errington Reay Weatherproof Pottery works. This superb Victorian Pipeworks enterprise is run by two brothers from their grandfather's business. They switched in 1974 to the current Errington Reay Weatherproof Pottery enterprise centred around one large kiln. My wife found it irresistible and we now are the proud owners of several fine pots!

Pass down the station approach and along the platform

(don't cross the line at this point). A footpath leading beyond the platform joins the road at a wicket-gate. Cross the line right, via the facing railway-gates, and follow the walled lane passing the camping field. The river ford is barred, but walkers have a fine footbridge spanning a broad reach of the River South Tyne. Once across bear right along the minor road, passing the entrance to Partridge Nest Farm, set pleasingly on a knoll, the name suggestive of the importance of game birds. It can be matched by the hamlet across the river Henshaw, which means 'hen wood'.

The road leads on for ¾ mile rising to Willimonteswick, the great corner gate-house tower forming an imposing feature on the approach. This was the birth-place of Bishop Nicholas Ridley who helped revise the liturgy under Edward VI. He was burnt at the stake, along with Latimer, at Balliol College in Oxford, for refusing to disavow his Protestant beliefs when Mary I assumed the throne, in 1555.

Pass through the farmyard, glancing to the right of the buildings via gates and slant down the open track. At the foot follow the fence into a fenced lane leading to Oadhall Mill. Long since shrunk to a country cottage retreat, farm vehicles are directed around the gated environs, while the footpath continues on through, via three gates. Respect the tenant's privacy. The track continues beyond the paddock to a fork. Ignore the descending track leading down to the water meadows, in winter, more waters than meadows. Bear left at a simple splashed waymark 'path' sign guiding up to a gate into Haughstrother Wood. Keep right on the undulating track through this fir tree bedecked hillside. Bring back the deciduous wood that must have preceded this coniferous invasion. Watch for the deer that by day stalk through this semi-dark world, a quiet footfall is necessary. Passing through the forestry-works clearing the track continues to exit below the replanted area, now advancing beside a beech and rhododendron bank, directly above the South Tyne.

The track sweeps left through a 'cleugh' via a gate returning to the fence above the wooded bank. Two further gates intervene and soon a footpath/track descending from High Barns is joined, descending to Shankfoot. Where shank means 'leg of land' and foot is precisely that! Pass through, crossing Howden Burn bridge bearing right onto the roadway leading from the farm, past cattle barns. This is the Unthank Road. The road runs under Howden Wood another conifer bank, rising under East Unthank farm to a cattle grid, now running alongside a wall, later above a conifer plantation.

Directly after East Lodge see the khaki tower left at the foot of a coal conveyor which runs under the road and across the river to a huge relay structure also painted in camouflage green. By this comparatively low-key mechanism coal from the open-cast workings on Plenmeller Common is despatched by train to power stations in the north-east. The quality of this coal is so good that apparently it is necessary to add clay to ease the burn. Does this sound curious? - the answer must be... yes!

The road now passes the old walled orchard, currently a sheltered paddock for a pony (notice the ornamental fountain in its midst) and sweeps up and round the back of Unthank Hall, which from this perspective has few charms. The house faces north-west enjoying a view along a straight reach of the South Tyne and therefore turns its back to the foot traveller. The charming little cottage adjacent, West Lodge, is a more likely cause for a second glance. The place-name comes from the Old English unpance' meaning 'without leave' and referred to a 'squatter's farm'. The road bends right and left to head due west towards the community of Plenmeller.

By now your thoughts might be on that cup of tea in Haltwhistle, but a moment's attention to the plantation up to the left, before you reach the end of the Unthank Road, is merited. In its midst is an Iron Age earthwork, which by some quirk of fate, or act of fact, lies at the Centre of Britain. The recent claim of the good burgesses of Haltwhistle that they reside at the very centre point of Britain is a cause for a little scrutiny of longitude and latitudes and a few other salient parameters beside (see final part of description). At the road junction notice the little building which would appear to have once been a school. The busy farm and newer farmhouse opposite is the residence of the owner of Unthank Hall, a diversified business of farming and large-scale forestry which extends into the Border Forests.

Go right along the road passing West Plenmeller Farm; notice the much modified bastle in the farmhouse. At the time of writing this piece the farm has just been sold, due to the imminent severance of land for the Haltwhistle by-pass, a cruel disfigurement of the valley and forfeit of the Tyne meadows.

Willimonteswick

CENTRE of BRITAIN?

Over recent years Haltwhistle has proclaimed to the traveller that it lies at the Heart of Roman Wall Country. A tongue-in-cheek phrase not well substantiated, especially in a town rooted firmly in the South Tyne valley, a seeming world away from the Roman Wall. Non-romantic eyes will view it as a small industrial town in the heart of the country. Nonetheless, the 'centralist' will find heart here. How neat for instance that it lies equidistant from Segedunum (Wallsend) and Maia (Bowness-on-Solway), 36½ miles. However, the matter does not stop there by a long chalk! If you run this 'centralist' idea around the compass you'll be astonished by the sequence of real distance coincidences that do occur. For instance look at longitude 2 degrees 26 minutes west, which touches the northern shore of North Ronaldsay, in Orkney and Portland Bill in Dorset, a distance of 290 miles. This is the longest line through Britain, and sure enough the halfway point is close at hand. If you look for the intersection of the latitude and longitudes - hey presto - they home in on a circular prehistoric earthwork sheltering in a plantation just to the south of the town, marked on the walk HIGHSPY VIEW.

Now take all the other main compass points from Haltwhistle and sure enough the landfalls have equidistant opposites. Taking this circular analogy on a stage, consider the official centre of England which is Meriden, tidal centre of dear ol' Blighty. Run your protractor round the arc and first you'll slice through the midst of Wales, then the tidal centres of Northern Ireland and Scotland. Take the fullest circle available and, yes, the tip of Jersey, Scilly Isles, Kerry and Shetland are equidistant from Haltwhistle. There are more reasons for belief than disbelief. There may be more in it than just pure measurement, but for the present I'm content to share the spirit of unity in our nation that this configuration attests to.

Coal conveyor crossing the South Tyne

As the road swings right notice the shallow valley left with its roadway and concealed industrial buildings. This is the largest plastic carton plant in Britain, BP Chemicals producing in the region of six million each week; by contrast with so many other chemical installations this is a masterly trick of landscaping.

The road next crosses the course of the old Alston Railway. At the time of writing, Roadlink have embarked upon the major task of building the Haltwhistle by-pass which will slice through the railway embankment and this minor road. So with little advice available on the eventual outcome walkers must pursue the most practical course current at the time of their visit. Currently one can follow Bellister Road to a footbridge over the South Tyne, from where the station platform left and town centre, under the railway bridge, are easily accessed.

I must admit to a huge sorrow in the need to violate this tract of meadow, made all the more sad when one considers the main part of the land belongs to the National Trust. It gives an unfortunate new meaning to the phrase 'taking the huff' - a haugh being raised ground in a water-meadow.

from LAMBLEY ____

6 mile circular walk featuring:
The SouthTyne Trail and the Maiden Way Roman road

Daffodils line the approach to Burnstones

START grid ref. NY 672584

Park in the broad space above
the village beside the A689.

The rectangular entrenchment immediately west, surveyed
over the gate, is the outline of a Dark Age homestead.
Although probably several centuries younger than the Milking
Gap settlement, it is but a vestige of the original farming
community from which Lambley evolved.

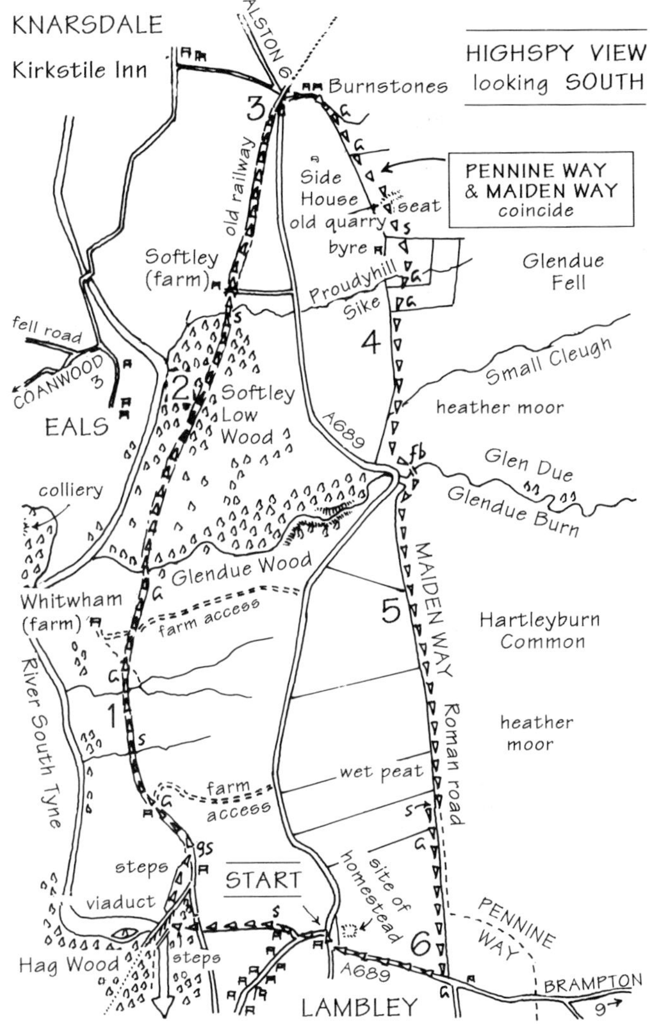

The place-name suggests that this locality was prized for its
lush spring pasture suitable to bring on the new crop of lambs

From Chapel Corner *either* descend the village street to join the path running right in sympathy with and just above the railway. Pass en route the 1885 parish church St Mary & St Patrick: a focus of high church ceremony, it is a rather special little church with a chancel that could grace many a 'grander' place of worship. Arthur Vaughan, priest from 1866-95, was instrumental in creating the vicarage and church, as well as the school and vicarage at Greenhead. Note the wall plaque to John Charlton, fellow of the Royal Meteorological Society - the climate of your thoughts is sure to reign in upon the impending weather!

Alternatively, and more directly, branch right 50 yards below Chapel Corner along the lane to Mendip (bungalow). Cross the stile and follow the metalled path with increasing gradient down to a wicket-gate, thus converging with the formerly mentioned path from the village. The natural progression along the trackbed is barred, necessitating a prompt descent via steps which formerly led to a metal footbridge bracketed onto the piers of the viaduct. Crumbling masonry and the safety of walkers galvanised action into dismantling it and the re-erection of a timber-framed structure the short distance downstream (however, this is not for us today). Upon reaching the first pier of the towering Lambley Viaduct, bear right within the fenced and stepped path ascending around the environs of the recently refurbished old Station House to a hand-gate.

The Haltwhistle to Alston branch line of the Carlisle to Newcastle Railway opened in 1852, with a further branch created from Lambley Station leading west to Brampton. The axe finally fell on these lines in 1976. Northumberland National Park is to be congratulated for establishing 12 miles of footpath along the track-bed to the Cumbria boundary at Gildersdale, 2 miles north of Alston. The loss of the railway service was dearly felt in Alston, the highest market town in England. A quirk of history set it in Cumberland (now Cumbria); geographically its allegiance has always been down the South Tyne, the railway having been a precious link with that world.

The trackbed is henceforward a province for walkers (and sheep!), and rightly so, providing a marvellous parade up the South Tyne valley, flanked by great swelling fells. Beyond two rather choicely sited and well-tended old railway cottages the trackbed crosses the re-aligned access to Waughold Holme. Passing through a gate, you may engage in rediscovering your natural brisk pace. Whitwham is an intriguing name and appears to mean 'sheltered place above a bend in the river'. Overlooking the farm see sited in the valley the hamlet of Eals, which appropriately means 'raised ground midst water meadows'.

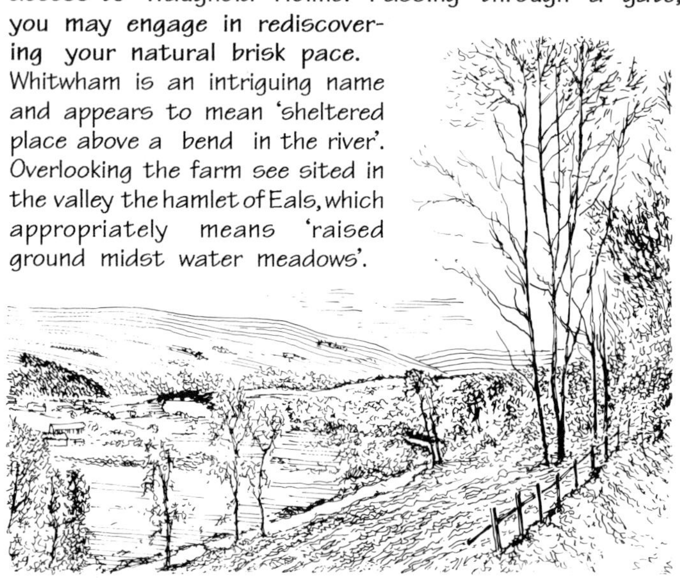

Eals backed by Wardley Law from the track in Softley Wood

A stile and three gates bring Glendue Viaduct impressively underfoot and a recently felled and brush-wood singed portion of Softley Low Wood. Glance through the fringing trees left across the valley, when the discreet workings of a small colliery in Towsbank Wood will be revealed. After three-quarters of a mile the delightful woodland passage ends at a stile. The route passes beneath the access bridge to Softley Farm. Softley here alludes to 'spongy ground', a commodity not in short supply during our traverse of Lambley Common. Only a simple fence stile to go before regretfully taking leave of the old South Tyne Railway. Should you have developed something of an affection for this old line, then resolve to visit the terminal station at Alston for a special nostalgic treat!

Greensward trackbed of the South Tyne Trail

Either join the A689 at the level opening or continue to the road bridge. Divert acutely right, down the retaining wall to join the road. The Kirkstile & Sportsman's Rest Inn at Knarsdale, where grouse-shooters and ramblers may mingle, is the mid-point prize of this walk. Much preferred to scrunched up sandwiches out of the day pack!

Branching west up the short lane to the handsome houses at Burnstones, the principal building was formerly an inn. Veer right rising with the track to the gate. Keeping beside the wall the track reaches a second gate then swings half left, guided by the Pennine Way sign right to slip through an old quarried hollow climbing to a simple seat. After a further 250 yards cross a ladder-stile, at the convergence with the Maiden Way. This Roman road came into existence during the pre-Wall forays of Julius Agricola, governor of Britannia 40-93 AD, during campaigns to advance Roman control to the Firth of Forth. Traverse the wild north Pennine range from Bravoniacum (Kirkby Thore) in the Eden valley to Magis (Carvoran), a Stanegate fort and staging-post to the northward route into Caledonian territory. Quite why damsels were associated with this 'way' is not recorded. Perhaps the answer lies in some folk-association beneath the Hanging Walls of Mark Anthony in the Eden valley where Roman sites at Kirkby Thore and on Stainmore share the name Maiden Castle.

The great expanse of Glendue Fell stretches west to the Pennine watershed culminating upon Cold Fell, the most northerly two thousand foot hill in the Pennine chain four wet moorland miles away. Fording Proudyhill Sike pass through successive gates on the gradual descent to Glen Due, 'the shady valley'. Although the valley road draws close to path, wayfarers sidestep it via a footbridge. The narrow way ascends beside the wall with the well managed heather moor of Hartleyburn Common flanking the path. The wall is replaced by a fence, the ridge flattens and soft peat replaces the firmer ground previously experienced along the Maiden Way. Coming alongside the grouse butts cross the stile, switching rather needlessly from the west to east side of the fence. After passing through a gate descend to a gate onto the road, en route bidding the Pennine Way farewell as it departs left at a stile mid-way down the fence. Follow the A689 for 600 yards to complete this pleasant adventure into deepest South Tynedale.

The Maiden Way entering Glen Due

Lambley Viaduct from near Yont the Cleugh

(below)
Towbank Colliery
semi-anthracite

Kirkstile Inn, Knarsdale

from GILSLAND

5½ mile circular walk featuring:
The Spa gorge, the Popping Stone and Crammel Linn

ROMAN GILSLAND:
Willowford bridge abutment and Milecastle 48

Crammel Linn

Helen and Daniel taking the waters at the Sulphur Spa Well

START grid ref. NY 634665

Leave Gilsland village street by the telephone kiosk and Bath House (see name fading on pale brick wall) where a signposted footpath directs north. The cinder path follows the true left bank of the River Irthing via two wicket-gates, passing the river stepping-stones after 600 yards.

It is pertinent to consider the water level, as the stones are crossed at the conclusion of the circuit - a pavement alternative exists down into Gilsland.

Thereafter, the well waymarked path crosses four stiles in passing through, and above Irthing House Farm, ascending a pasture bank to join the Wardrew Farm by-road. Advancing along this quiet road, cross the cattle-grid; go left where this forks on the approach to Wardrew House. Immediately after the road

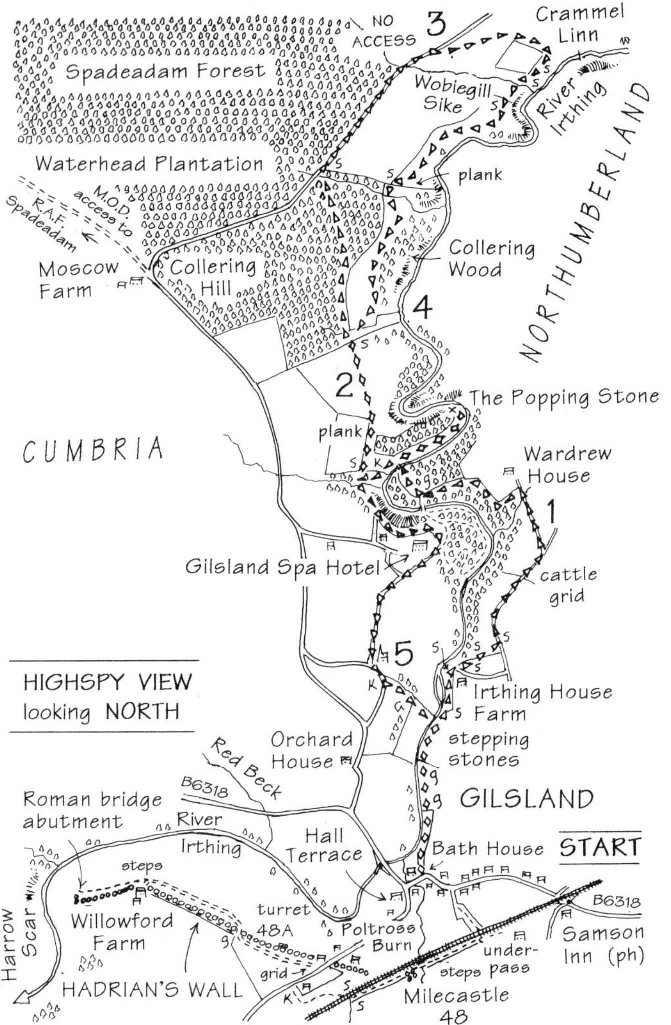
Spadeadam Forest
NO ACCESS
3
Crammel Linn
Wobiegill Sike
River Irthing
Waterhead Plantation
M.O.D. access to
R.A.F. Spadeadam
plank
Collering Wood
Moscow Farm
Collering Hill
NORTHUMBERLAND
4
CUMBRIA
2
The Popping Stone
plank
Wardrew House
1
Gilsland Spa Hotel
cattle grid
5
Irthing House Farm
HIGHSPY VIEW
looking NORTH
stepping stones
Orchard House
GILSLAND
Red Beck
B6318
Roman bridge abutment
River Irthing
Hall Terrace
Bath House
START
steps
turret 48A
Poltross Burn
B6318
Harrow Scar
Willowford Farm
grid
under-steps pass
Samson Inn (ph)
HADRIAN'S WALL
Milecastle 48

dips, crossing a small re-entrant beck, follow the sign-posted path left beside the old metal fence and above the wooded scarp. Keep round, right, between pasture and woodland, with Wardrew House plainly in view to the right. The present house dates from the early eighteenth century and as a hotel was visited by Robert Burns in 1787 and ten years later by Sir Walter Scott. Formerly the site of a steading belonging to the de Thirlwalls.

 Proceed downhill, to the left along the recently drained track, to reach the Woodland Trust hand-gate on the right. Take the opportunity to briefly cross the footbridge ahead to inspect the Spa Well (rebuilt in 1964) ; the trickling spout issues an authentic sulphurous flow. Though nasally repulsive the sparkling mineral water has, from Roman times, been appreciated for its health giving properties, affording relief from an array of ailments. The impressive wooded gorge can be well comprehended from this spot. During its nineteenth century heyday, before all was lost to a landslip, this was the location of a cluster of Spa entertainment pavilions.

 Backtrack over the footbridge, to pass through the hand-gate, advancing beside the fence to a second footbridge, with new perspectives of the wooded gorge. Once across turn right, following the waymarked path upstream (not a definitive footpath, despite the signing) passing the flood rock debris filled river coming to a conclusive halt at The Popping Stone: admire the ravine beyond (no path). The Irthing is seen emerging from the sinuous cragbound ravine, a place to linger if ever there was. In fact, it is local folklore that Sir Walter Scott, during his stay in 1797 indulging in spa health society, not only met his future wife, Miss Carpentier, but promptly proposed to her at this evidently conducively seductive location...

... does it have the necessary romantic ambience for you?

 Backtrack, passing the footbridge to rise via an amorously appropriate 'kissing' gate into a wooded re-entrant. At the acute bend, branch right, footpath

The Popping Stone

sign 'Butterburn Road', ascending the narrow path to a fence stile at the top of the bank. Follow the fence north with a fine view right. Passing above a conifer enclosure, continue to a simple plank bridge adjacent to an intriguing glimpse into The Popping Stone gorge. Angle half left on a post waymarked path through the rushy pasture to a ladder-stile over the wall. From this spot we embark upon a part permitted path loop to admire the picturesque charm of Crammel Linn waterfall.

Follow the footpath half left keeping the broken wall to the right, ascending to where a waymark post directs half left along the broad rushy avenue between the young conifers. Reaching a stile join the open road. Turn right enjoying the broad views of moor and forest spotting to the north-east Winshields Crag, highest point on the Whin Sill, and therefore of Hadrian's Wall. The plantation right has recently been clear felled. Together with the tall conifers of Waterhead Plantation to the left this land belongs to the 6500 acre Spadeadam Forest, part of the huge 250 sq. mile Forestry Commission 'Border Forest Park'.

East Cumbria Countryside Project strategic waymark post

Crossing a cattle grid and dipping across Wobiegill Sike, leave the road right, at the lay-by, opposite the powerline terminal post.

The large intentionally intimidating notice confirms that all this ground belongs to the Ministry of Defence. As an RAF electronic warfare training range it is subjected to periodic mock attacks from aircraft seeking to defy radar

The Irthing below Crammel Linn

detection. When the red flag is hoisted this is not a comfortable place to linger! Secreted in the dark depths of the forest the military establishment was formerly used as both launch-pad for the Blue Streak rocket project and to test the fatigue limits of helicopter rotor-blades.
  Follow the marshy path, courtesy of the Defence Council, with the occasional sleeper plank easing footing to the corner of a fenced enclosure. Descend beside the fence to the foot of the enclosure. To the east admire the fine prospect of the often roaring Crammel Linn. Forming the county boundary between Cumbria and Northumberland the Irthing emerges on a long sinuous journey from its birth in the lonely moorland wastes above Spadeadam Forest. Crammel Linn may derive its name from either 'the spout frequented by herons' or 'the cauldron falls'; this latter is more likely, being an anglo-Gaelic corruption.

The permissive path angles right to reach a stile and fenced passage above the river. After the next stile the path curves west to ford Wobiegill Sike. Guided by way-marks, it rises to a fence stile, contouring above the scenic meanderings of the Irthing. Following a plank bridge the path bears right to a wall stile, then dips through a hollow crossing a burn, thereafter keeping right above Collering Wood before descending and rising to regain the ladder-stile to complete a loop. Retrace your steps southward to the re-entrant path. Now ascend right admiring the excellent views into the wooded gorge to pass close by Gilsland Spa Hotel. Established in 1901 as a convalescent home by a group of northern Co-operative Societies, it is now run as a family holiday hotel by the Co-op. From the car park follow the road to the road junction beside St. Mary Magdalene Episcopalian Church, built in 1854, in simple Early English style, exclusively for Spa resort clientele.

Following the pavement turn left, then left again at the kissing-gate. The path descends the bank via a mid-course gate to the stepping-stones over the river Irthing. At times of spate do not leave the road, instead return to the village along the roadside path.

Mumps Ha' incorporated
within Hall Terrace

ROMAN GILSLAND

Visitors to Gilsland wishing to see the Roman Wall should proceed south from the Bridge Inn junction, passing Hall Terrace. Within the fabric of the upper portion of this terrace survives the notorious hostelry, Mumps Ha' (notice the blocked windows), referred to in Sir Walter Scott's novel 'Guy Mannering'. In the seventeenth century the proprietress of Mumps Ha' was known to give succour to brigands at a time when travellers and honest country-folk were daunted by the activities of such free-booters, making Gilsland a place to avoid rather than the merry resort it became.

Proceed upon the pavement passing Raise House and Roman Way, the former vicarage, its current dire state a needless visual trauma. A small gate on the left gives access to the consolidated length of Roman Wall leading east. This can be inspected, noting the culvert draining the shallow hollow. Return to the road, go left and right, crossing the cattle-grid at the entrance to Willowford Farm. Follow the access track beside the length of well re-constructed Wall; notice that the Narrow Wall rests upon Broad Wall foundations. Take the opportunity to inspect Turret 48a (see panel).

Turret 48a

Where the farm road switches through the Wall into the north ditch, continue through the wicket-gate, keeping to the south side of the Wall to Willowford Farm.

This eighteenth century farm was built from the Wall's ruin beside Turret 48b. A small charge is levied at the farm because the access path beside the monument leading down to the Roman bridge abutment carries no legal right of way. The visitor has no access to the river bank, some 60 yards distant from the stranded abutment. Until thirty years ago a private aerial ropeway existed enabling Wall-pilgrims to haul themselves across to the far bank, where they could climb Harrow Scar regaining the Wall's course at Milecastle 49.

Within the plan for the National Trail it is proposed to erect a footbridge to effect continuity to Harrow Scar and Birdoswald. An information panel details the development of the Roman bridge. It appears a mill-race operated powering a corn-mill. Floods damaged the earlier stuctures, later work involving the creation of a high ramp and chariotway.

Retracing your approach to the public road, turn right, passing Gilsland Primary School, go through the kissing-gate on the left. Proceed via the plank bridge then bear half left across the pasture to ascend the incline to the stiles at the railway crossing - a moment for extreme caution! Follow the fenced passage left leading to the Poltross Burn Milecastle 48 enclosure. Revealed within the sloping interior is a layout of buildings and gates: in the north-east corner is the base of steps which led to the Wall-walk (information panel).

Descend the footpath steps to Poltross Burn footbridge, deftly switching from Cumbria into Northumberland. Ascend the opposing steps, go left through the railway underpass via the play ground to re-enter Gilsland village street, turn left to conclude a fascinating and beautiful walking experience.

from BIRDOSWALD ____

7 mile linear walk featuring:
Traces of the Roman road and
Signal Station, Holy Well sulphur spring, Bewcastle
Roman Fort, Castle, Anglian Cross and Lime Kiln Inn

The serpentine Irthing from the southern brink of Birdoswald

START grid ref. NY 616664

Begin from the visitor car park at Birdoswald. Walk uphill as to the fort entrance. Opposite the fort's north gate a gate right gives access to the pasture. From this spot a bridle-way sets course initially preserving the course of the unnamed Roman road to Bewcastle. Bridle-gates were installed in Spring 1994, facilitating the traverse of Midgeholme Moss, which is a deep peat basin. It must have been more like a tarn in Roman times,

West gate of Birdoswald Roman Fort

which makes it all the more surprising that the road engineers did not bend their bee-line rules to allow a drier start via Kiln Hill. Reaching the road, go right and left at the field-gate embarking upon a greenway that has all the hall-marks of a Roman causeway. Continue via two gates into rougher pasture, maintain course to a bridle-gate into the dauntingly tussocky fringe of Waterhead Common Plantation. For ease of walking perhaps the indiscretion of clambering over the forest bounding fence left may be condoned, advancing through the marshy hollow of Trencher Beck before ascending the shallow ridge and placing yourself back on the approved side of the fence. Go through a bridle-gate at the forest corner. I might add that the author facing all hardship stayed inside the forest fence and can offer no solace to anyone hell bent on holding stoically to the correct line.

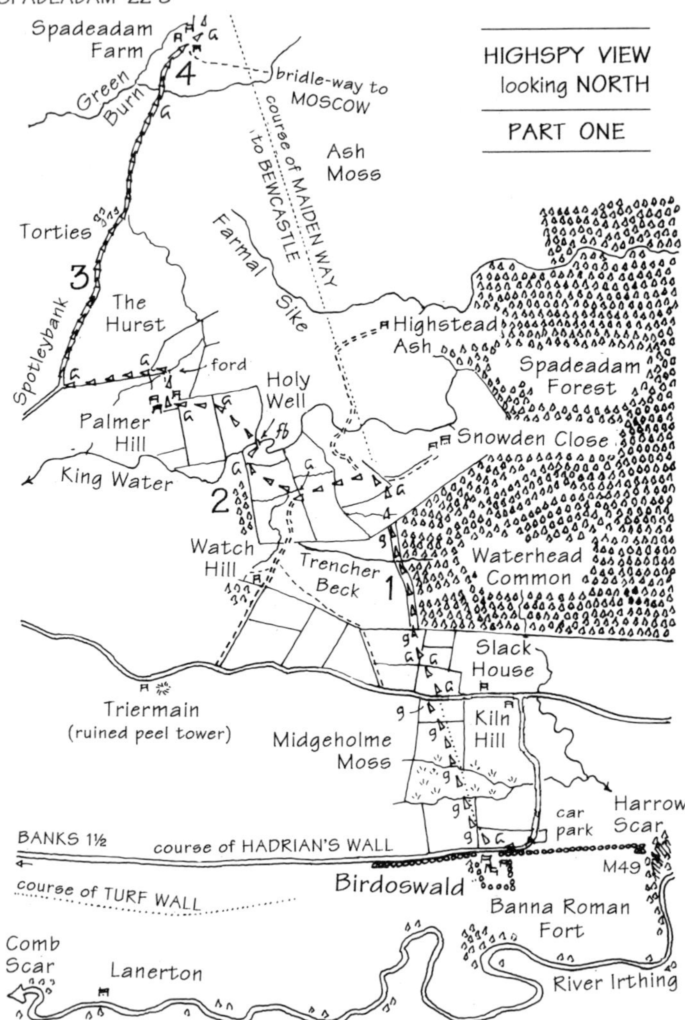

SPADEADAM 22-3
Spadeadam Farm
Green Burn
4
bridle-way to MOSCOW
course of MAIDEN WAY to BEWCASTLE
Ash Moss
HIGHSPY VIEW looking NORTH
PART ONE
Torties
3
Spotleybank
The Hurst
Farmal Sike
Highstead Ash
Spadeadam Forest
ford
Holy Well
fb
Palmer Hill
Snowden Close
King Water
2
Watch Hill
Trencher Beck
1
Waterhead Common
Slack House
Triermain
(ruined peel tower)
Midgeholme Moss
Kiln Hill
car park
Harrow Scar
BANKS 1½
course of HADRIAN'S WALL
Birdoswald
M49
course of TURF WALL
Banna Roman Fort
Comb Scar
Lanerton
River Irthing

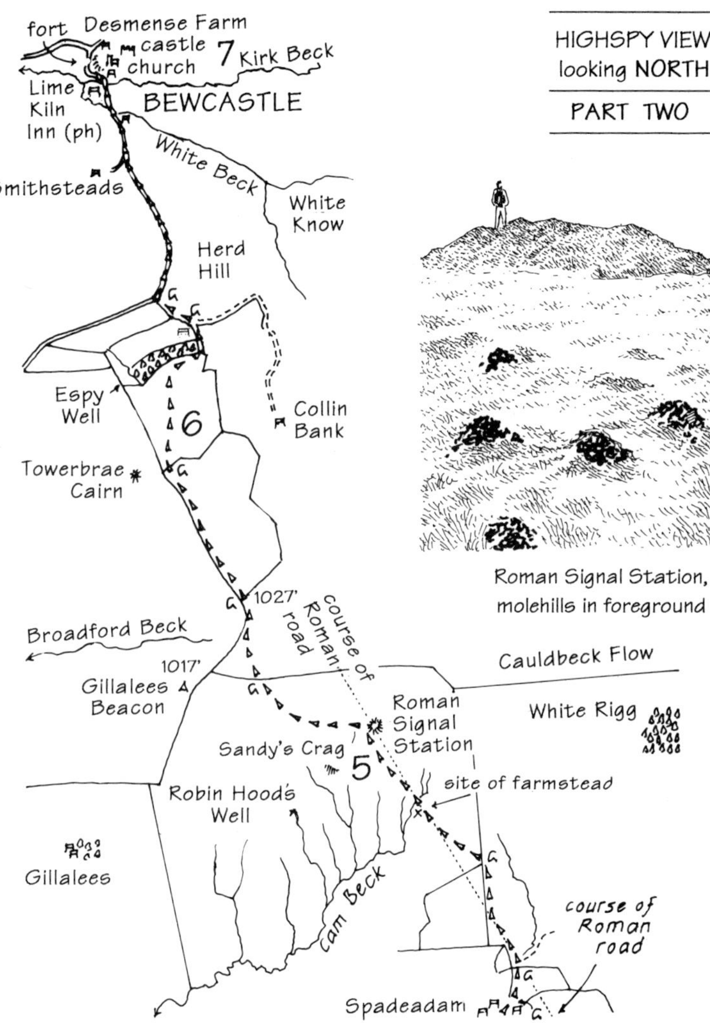

HIGHSPY VIEW
looking **NORTH**

PART TWO

Roman Signal Station,
molehills in foreground

Perhaps matters will improve with use - but only perhaps! Passing through the broken wall directly after the bridle-gate advance across the ditch noticing ahead the tell-tale groove of the Roman road where the pasture slopes away northwards. Keep right to reach a gate in the corner where the fence and hedge meet (the Roman way being lost on the descent). Descend beside the hedge to join the concrete road beside the 'Snowden Close' sign. Forsake the Roman road by going left along the roadway over a cattle-grid, admire the beech avenue on the right. Passing through the next gateway angle right to a fence gate, bear half left traversing the pasture to a fence gate beside the wall, descend towards the light woodland seeking a narrow path bearing right, down to a footbridge in the little King Water gorge. Just before crossing the gorge,

The Holy Well

notice the moss covered steps leading down to a rock alcove where sulphureous water issues from a fissure. Known as the Holy Well this tiny mineral spring has largely been forgotten since Gilsland's heyday as a Victorian resort, when this fairy glen will have been a cherished excursion. It formerly served the Augustinian canons of Lanercost Priory who traipsed the ten miles to celebrate St John the Baptist's Day each 24th June, a veneration that included a water blessing ceremony. The footbridge is scheduled for renewal. No doubt when you reach this spot, your thoughts will turn nostalgically upon what

King Water at the Holy Well footbridge

perilous rotting span the author had crossed, for by then the matter will have surely been resolved. Suffice to say that if I had been foolish enough to have closed my eyes I would have slipped through the middle and made one heck of a splash, and this book might not have seen the light of day!

From the footbridge the footpath goes left, crossing a minor stream, before bearing right up the bank onto the pasture aiming half left to a galvanised gate in the fence, progressing to a second galvanised gate beside a dutch barn at Palmer Hill (farm). Beyond the barn go right, descending the unenclosed access track, sweeping left through a cobbled ford and via the gate. Progressing beside the wall to a gate onto the

Spadeadam Farm

minor road, go right for nearly 1½ miles on a switch-back beeline bound for Spadeadam Farm via one road gate.

The nineteenth century architecture of Spadeadam farmhouse (datestone 1862) is reminiscent of Thirlwall Castle Farm, the protruding gable a distinctive feature. The original farmhouse is disguised in the barn close to the farm track.   Ignore the bridle-way signed 'Moscow', instead pass straight through the farmyard swinging left via gates onto an open track.

After 150 yards pass a star marker indicating the proximity of sensitive archaeological remains: in this instance referring to the Roman road and signal station on Beacon Hill. Ignore the bridle-way sign 'Shopford Road', pass through the ensuing galvanised gate, do not be lured by the wayward course of the open track (of only agricultural significance), nor ford the burn. Instead keep company with the fence run-ning north, at this point aligned to the hypothesised course of the Roman road (no visible trace). Continue from the fence corner over cattle muddied ground rising parallel to the wall to find a recently re-newed gate in the wall above the junction of walls. Follow the ditch feature rising half right, at the first beck crossing. Evidence for the old farmstead indicated on the Pathfinder map is spartan. Keep a north-westerly course in sympathy with the Roman road to visit the Roman Signal Station.

The earthwork offers little scope for investigation, having received a thorough desecration in the last century leaving all stonework re-clamped. This was a significant site high on the south flank of Gillalees Beacon. Roman scouts on military reconnaissance duty, strategically based at the Bewcastle outpost fort, will have conveyed intelligence on barbarian movements, by this simple form of early warning semaphore, to the defenders of the Wall. The fire beacon will have been seen by keen eyes from Vercovicium to Maia (Housesteads to Bowness-on-Solway) and turned normal

Discarded in the marsh above the Signal Station is this fading notice from the long departed days of 'Blue Streak' research

amber alert to red alert in quick time. Evidence of the Roman road is sketchy on the sphagnum moor beyond the station.

There are few features to this hillside to cause the walker to divert, though Sandy's Crag a short way south of the mound is curiously pock-marked and may have been exploited as a Roman quarry. An adjacent, otherwise nondescript, spring bears the common outlaw name Robin Hood's Well - Kevin Costner didn't come here as far as I know!

The bridleway continues to a gate in the fence, immersed in the ridge marsh. The nearby O.S. column (S6503) at Gillalees Beacon is a fine viewpoint, notably west to the Solway.

Joining the ridge wall leading north pass through a gate at the high point of Tower Brae, thereon the bridleway follows the wall on a gradual descent. From the next gate, notice Towerbrae Cairn, the tumulus over the wall to the left, and admire the prospect ahead over the valley of Kirk Beck centred on Bewcastle. The indistinct bridle-way drifts slightly right on the steepening descent, keeping right of the emerging re-entrant hollow to pick up a discernible track which runs down beside the scarp woodland to a new bungalow and a gate. Joining the track from Collin Bank go left to the gate onto the minor road. Go right to conclude the walk via the Lime Kiln Inn. It may only be of historic relevance by the time you read this commentary, but beside the track leading east to the distant dwelling at High Grains, below Whitebeck Cottage, stands (or stood) a hen-house converted into Bewcastle's very own Post Office! Open Monday to Saturday 8.45 - 11 a.m.; it must be unique. In an age paranoid with a need for security, one can appreciate concern for the post-mistress' safety in such an exposed spot, indeed robbers could scoop the whole coop!

Bewcastle is a scattered community holding special

Bewcastle Post Office in 1993, with Dick Dickson the postman on his round en route from High Grains, arguably the loneliest house in Cumbria. Is the hen house post office the most primitive of its genre in England ?

appeal, perhaps more so because it lies remote, in the bleak northern extremity of Cumbria. Walkers' attention will be drawn beyond the pub to the raised ground above Kirk Beck, where the parish church stands within the Roman fort and adjacent to the hanging walls of a Norman castle built by Beuth, who declared himself 'Lord of Bewcastle Dale'.

The Romans first adapted the convenient shelf for their outpost fort, the remains are clearly defined. Climb the bank directly from the cattle grid to gain the rampart corner. The parish church and rectory stand on the southern area of the fort; notice the shallow baulks of the barrack blocks in the open pasture north of the churchyard entrance. If you glance over the field wall adjacent to them the rough surface of the paddock betrays the outline of the headquarters and associated buildings. The crumbling walls of the Norman castle rise beyond (entry and descriptive leaflet from Mrs Noble at Demense Farm) dating from the reign of Edward I. In 1567 they were recorded as being in a state of disrepair, now only assailed by cattle. They stand in the north-east corner of the fort with a moat cut into the fort's interior.

Enter St Cuthbert's churchyard, packed with memorial headstones, some 'taller than a man'. The piece-de-resistance without question is Bewcastle Cross, a headless sandstone shaft standing over fourteen feet high. This master-piece of seventh century carving is acclaimed as a major sculpted relic of that period. Yet mystery surrounds its locational authenticity. The lack of contemporary finds in the vicinity suggests that the cross was 'acquired' from a pair at Rothwell, near Dumfries. The transfer perhaps co-incided with a thirteenth century desire to elevate the fledgling manorial market at Bewcastle. See the leaflets available in the church and inspect the Bewcastle Past & Present exhibition, open 9 a.m. to dusk, in the barn adjacent to the rectory.

Twelve information panels give succinct insight upon the history of this lonely farming community, examining Bewcastle's prehistory, giving evidence of settlement back to 4000 B.C. from cists and cairns within the parish. The unusual six-sided Roman fort is given special prominence, including a plan and various artefacts found during the site excavations during the late 1930s, 1950s and 1970s. Also featured are the crumbling ruins of the castle, a target for Scottish raids. No wonder it lies waste. The Anglian Cross which pre-dates the castle by perhaps three hundred years is inscribed with runic inscriptions that on its west side translates thus:

> "This slender victory sign set up HWAETRED, WOTHGAR, OLWFWOL THU, in memory of ALCFRITH a king and son of Oswin. Pray for his soul."

Anglian Cross, Bewcastle churchyard

from CHAPELBURN ————————————————————————

returning via:
Banks 4½ miles
Gunshall 3 miles
Lanerton 2½ miles

Three options for a circular walk featuring:
The wooded gorge surrounding Comb Crag with its
Roman quarry, Wall turrets 51a and 51b
and Pike Hill Signal Station

The Irthing gorge below Comb Crag

START grid ref. NY 596645

The most entertaining circular walk in this sector of Wall
Country begins from Chapelburn on the south bank of the
Irthing, some 5 miles east of Brampton. This tiny community
lies upon Stanegate where the Romans built a marching

camp prior to the establishment of their great Wall, the earthwork lying close to the church. The walk which includes the WALL WALK from Appletree to Banks has three options, each founded upon the superb Comb Crag gorge.

via BANKS Park on the broad verge of the Gilsland to Low Row road, a few yards west of the lane to St.Cuthbert's Church. Walk east along the road through the hamlet, turn left after Chapelburn Farmhouse, datestone 1672.

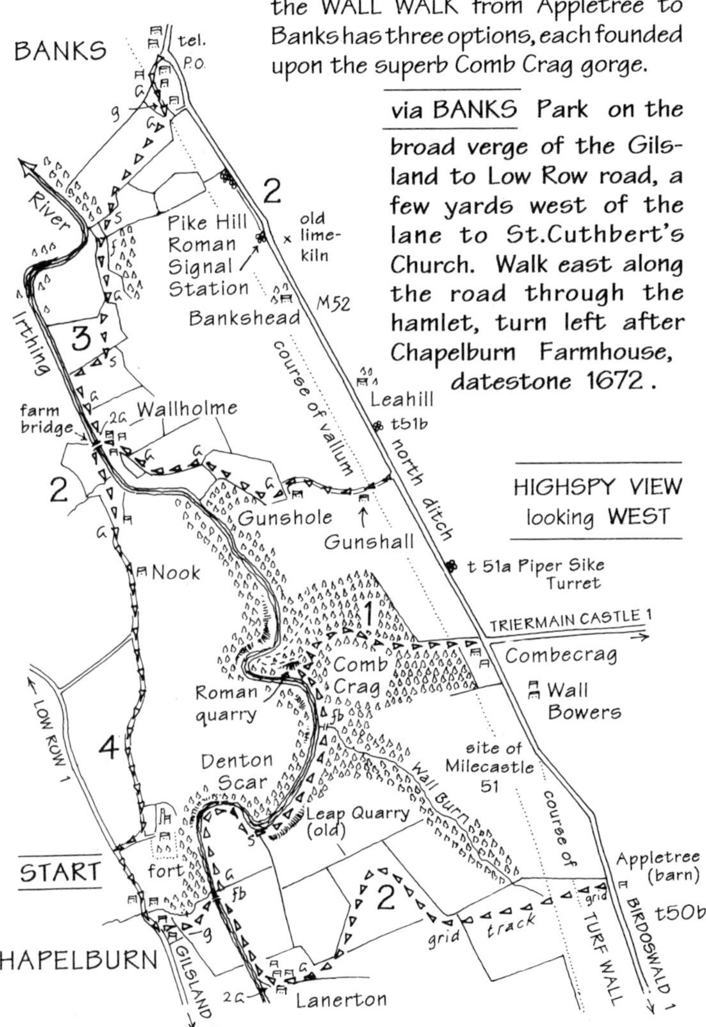

Chapelburn Farmhouse

Go left beside the holiday cottage and down the garden to a bridle-gate. Continue down the pasture bank, taking a sideways look at the charming embowered waterfall in Chapel Burn, to reach what must be one of the most impressive suspension footbridges in all Cumbria; built in 1986 by the County Council at a cost of £28,000, it is amazing this bridle-way is not waymarked off the road to encourage use of this expensive piece of iron-work. Presumably horse-riders nonetheless are expected to ford!

Waterfall in Chapel Burn

Irthing falls where the path enters the gorge

From the suspension bridge go left, through the gate, keeping to the riverbank as it sweeps beneath Denton Scar and the site of the Stanegate fort. Anticipation mounts as the peat darkened river spills over a shallow fall and the path enters the wooded Comb Crag gorge via a stile. When first I walked this way in 1989 the first thirty yards were a dangerous balancing act upon slippery slabs tight to the river's edge. That situation has been remedied by the efforts of the East Cumbria Countryside Project and volunteers, by the building of a substantial causeway; nature will have to work hard to mellow the concrete to fit it to this beautiful scene.

Footbridge over Wall Burn

Whilst users of this guide will welcome the easier access, there lingers a compelling argument for repelling greater pedestrian visitation within so charming a sanctuary. Please respect this repose. The path passes on a switch-back course, beneath the long abandoned Leap Quarry. Cross the intriguing fissured bedrock Wall Burn, via the picturesque single arched bridge. With sumptuous views down upon cataracts and crags, the whole richly wooded setting has all the romance of an equatorial rain forest. Indeed, it comes as no surprise to appreciate that the RSPB treasures this place, and holds a management agreement with the owners, therefore walkers must pass quietly, being sensitive of its status as a bird sanctuary.

Like a defiant finger, a hard band of sandstone has caused the river to prize a way through, twisting sharply south and north. The footpath is also forced abruptly north by the arete, rising above a Roman quarry. Low down on a tilted rock-wall in the quarry the following Roman inscription can be discovered :

> 'SECVRVS', IVSTVS', 'MATHRIANVS' and 'FAVST ET RVF COS'
> translation: Faustinus and Rufus were Consuls in 210 A.D.

The rock cutting is adorned with a welter of etched initials and apparently frivolous inscriptions, the earliest being 'Wood-Warden 1850'. Walkers may descend the beautiful arete, following the path right at the foot of the ridge. However, this footpath very soon turns back ascending to rejoin the principal path beneath a yew tree.

Ridge-top path on Comb Crag

The main path leaves the rock cutting westwards, passing a noble redwood just after the junction with the lower path. It rises out of the scarp woodland into a felled area where the clearly marked path runs north between the Combcrag Wood and a field wall, dipping through the line of the Vallum, before joining the road at 'Combecrag Farm' (spelling as per farm sign). From the Combecrag road junction head left (west) following the minor road towards Banks. En route pass the revealed turrets 51a and 51b. Originally built for the Turf Wall, neither have the usual wings for the later bonding into the stone Wall.

Milecastle 52 is lost beneath the farm buildings at Banks-head: from 1924 to her death in 1981 Bankshead was the home of the celebrated Cumbrian water-colourist Winifred Nicholson.

Eventually the road walking is rewarded by the arrival of Pike Hill Signal Station. The road has encroached into the tower, which stands askew to the line of the Wall. Being associated with the earlier Stanegate system this signal station pre-dates the building of the Wall, but probably continued to serve as a Wall observatory. The view is unquestionably fine, from the Nine Nicks of Thirlwall above Greenhead to the east; across the southern arc of northern Pennine heights featuring Cold Fell and the headwaters of the Gelt; to the magical tangle of Lakeland fells. Keener eyes than mine have claimed that Scafell Pike is visible through the gap formed by Clough Head and Souther Fell; and on round to Criffell across the Solway; Chapelcross Power Station near Annan; the Lockerbie Hills featuring the flat-topped Burnswark; with Spadeadam Forest forming the northern horizon. No wonder the Romans adopted this vantage as a target for their Wall, albeit that it put the natural moat of the Irthing behind, rather than to the fore of their marshal line.

Lime-kiln on Pike Hill

Follow the path down to the short length of Wall connected to turret 52a. Shortly thereafter, the road walk ends upon entry into Banks. Turn left after Banks Post Office, passing the telephone box on the Green, then turning left again via a red gate into the lane leading towards Glen Wood.

Before reaching the bungalow branch right into the pasture through a wicket-gate and a field-gate, in order to descend the pasture. Slant diagonally left down the field, seeking a stile in the fence in the vicinity of the transition from pasture to light woodland. This path maintains its downward course to a second simpler stile - barbed wire wrapped with a fertilizer bag! Carefully negotiate the loose strands of wire in passing through light woodland, prone to boggy patches - thanks to the occasional visitation by cattle. On reaching the make-shift gate into the valley pasture cross to a stile, follow the hedge right, to the River Irthing. The path accompanies the riverside track, via a gate, to Wallholme.

via GUNSHALL

From the Combecrag road junction go left (west). Follow the road, passing the remains of turret 51a, turn left down the lane, sign-posted 'Gunshole Farmhouse' and 'Gunshall' (no foot path waymarking). A gate right, just before entry into the bottom farmyard at Gunshall, puts the footpath on course to descend the two fields. Keep the hedge to the left, via two gates and through Wallholme farmyard to the Irthing bridge.

Chapelburn can be reached via the unenclosed metalled road linking Wallholme with the outside world. Don't hasten past the lonely St.Cuthbert's Church, overlooking the site of the Roman fort (now under arable cropping); of particular interest is the recently discovered Roman altar standing forlornly outside the porch.

<u>via LANERTON</u> From the Combecrag road junction go right (east) along the by-road founded upon Hadrian's Wall. To the left of the road, notice the course of the stone Wall's north ditch. Until the turn of the nineteenth century the stone Wall was coveted by all manner of builders; the rubble core presumably rests as the hardcore of the road itself. After 'Wall Bowers' glance right to see the convergent Turf Wall ditch and bank, at the site of Milecastle 51. On reaching the attractively named Apple-tree barn, turn right following the unenclosed farm track signed 'Lanerton'. At the head of Wall Burn the track cuts through the line of the Turf Wall and vallum. After crossing the cattle-grid enjoy the fine view south to Cold Fell, the most northern 2000 foot fell in the Pennine chain. The farm track winds down to Lanerton Farm. In common with Lanercost, Lanerton appears to derive its name from the Welsh 'llanerch', thereby translating to 'the farmstead within a glade'. The handsome vernacular farmhouse merits a glance. Continue through the gates and along the riverbank to the suspension bridge, retracing your footsteps up to Chapelburn.

Remnants of Pike Hill signal station, angled at 45 degrees to the Wall

St.Cuthbert's, Chapelburn built on the site of a Stanegate fort

from LANERCOST BRIDGE ________________________________

4 mile circular walk featuring:
Lanercost Priory and Hadrian's Wall west from Hare Hill

Gatehouse to Naworth Castle

START grid ref. NY 554634

Park at Lanercost Bridge. From this delectable spot in
the Irthing valley, seemingly remote from Hadrian's Wall's
irresistible westward march for the Solway lowlands, walkers
can either combine the fine stretch of Wall dyke from Hare
Hill accompanying its much diminished traces west to
Howgill, or they can opt for a much shorter stroll, which will
also reward visitors to Lanercost Priory, by satisfying their
desire to 'set foot upon the Wall' by walking up the bridle-

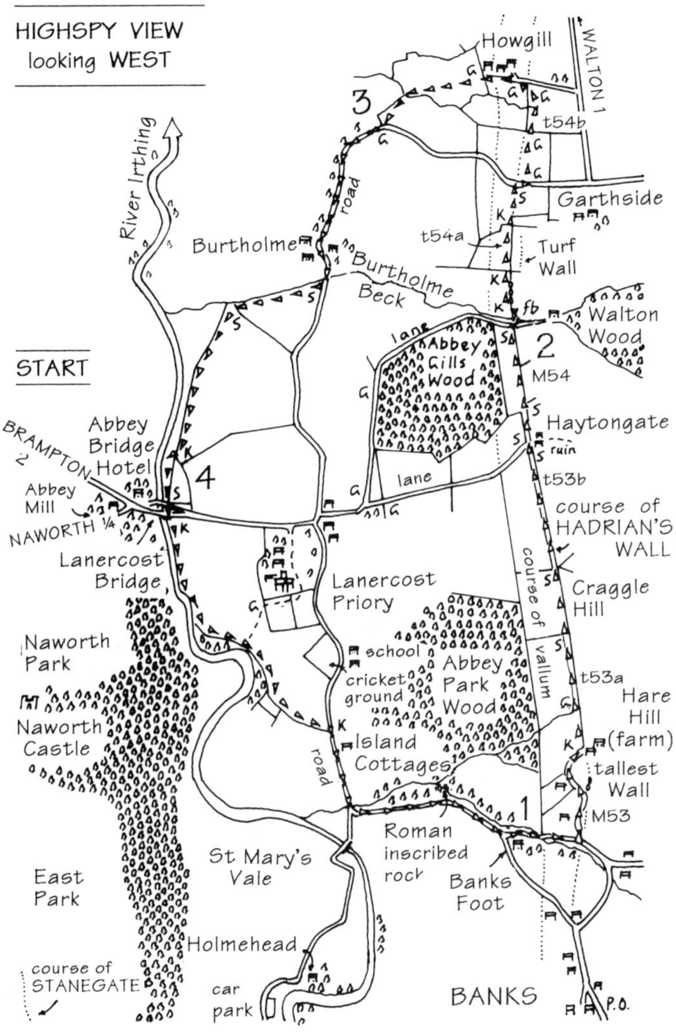
HIGHSPY VIEW
looking WEST
START
River Irthing
Howgill
WALTON 1
t54b
Garthside
Burtholme
Burtholme Beck
t54a
Turf Wall
Walton Wood
lane
Abbey Gills Wood
2
M54
Haytongate
ruin
t53b
course of HADRIAN'S WALL
Craggle Hill
course of vallum
lane
BRAMPTON 2
Abbey Bridge Hotel
Abbey Mill
NAWORTH ¼
4
Lanercost Bridge
Lanercost Priory
Naworth Park
school
cricket ground
Abbey Park Wood
t53a
Hare Hill (farm)
Naworth Castle
Island Cottages
tallest Wall
M53
East Park
St Mary's Vale
Roman inscribed rock
Banks Foot
1
course of STANEGATE
Holmehead
car park
BANKS
P.O.
fb

Abbey Bridge Hotel

lane which leads north to Hayton Gate, backtracking from Abbey Gill Wood. This latter, inner walk may serve as a means of curtailment of the longer excursion, should dark clouds threaten or your brisk step falter!

Lanercost Bridge

Part romantic ruin, part the beautiful parish church of St Mary Magdalene, the original Lanercost Priory plundered dressed stone directly from the Wall to create an elegant medieval masterpiece. From late 1306 Edward I convalesced here for six months, naturally with full court in attendance: the nation's government was therefore directed from this furthest outpost of England.

Lanercost Priory from the north-west

Pass through the kissing-gate on the east side of Abbey Bridge, to follow the riverbank footpath up-stream. The path is deflected from the broad meander of the Irthing as the river sweeps past the Priory to continue beside the hedge via a second kissing-gate onto the road. Turn right. Keeping on the pavement pass Island Cottages, continue along the road curving north at the Low Row turn. Passing the lay-by the road steepens: at the first bend glance over the white rails into the ravine to reveal a rock slab bearing a cryptic Roman inscription. Unfortunately the inscription is not visible from this range and the newly planted gill banks afford no public access. At Banks Foot, where the road forks, go left, to enjoy the sylvan company of Banks Burn. Shortly after the road slices through the 'lost' vallum turn left up the access lane to Hare Hill Farm. As the lane bends look right to the famous nine foot high section of Hare Hill Wall close to the site of Milecastle 53.

In 1802 William Hutton commented 'I viewed this relic with admiration ... I saw no higher'. It was the highest piece of original Wall, however, its consolidation this century necessitating a total re-building. The initials 'PP' are inscribed at mid-height, on the north face, at the eastern end of the Wall. This centurial stone refers to a 'primus pilus' or senior centurion of a cohort, responsible for this section of Wall construction.

Seventeen courses of Roman Wall masonry on Hare Hill

Ascend beyond this well tended stretch of Wall, locating the kissing-gate just prior to the entrance to Hare Hill Farm. Passing below the farm enjoy the fine southerly views across the Irthing valley to Tindale, Cold, Talkin and Cumrew Fells, the northernmost prow of the Pennine Range. A kissing-gate lures the walker into a dairy cow gang-way running alongside the line of the Wall whilst passing the invisible site of turret 53a. Thereafter, a series of stiles assists progress by the Wall, with dressed Wall base stones evident. Continue over Craggle Hill, which means 'hill frequented by heron (crane)', passing another intangible turret, 53b. There are splendid views north towards Spadeadam, west to Criffel across the Solway Firth; west-north-west to the distinctive hills near Lockerbie, notably the distinctive 'table-topped' Burnswark Hill; while to the south-west Blencathra and Skiddaw form a tantalising diversion for the eye. This passage of Wall country, bowling through undulating hills with nothing more than the north ditch to hint to the frontier, has much of the 'flavour' of certain stretches of Offa's Dyke through the Welsh Marches. Bird-song rings in the wind, making this one of the most relaxing passages of the entire WALL WALK. At Haytongate, restored as the home of a craftsman in wood, a bridle-lane leads left (south) directly down to Lanercost Priory.

Course of Hadrian's Wall at Walton Wood

Progressing via wooden ladder-stiles descend beside the Wall bank, passing the site of Milecastle 54. Cross the stile at the foot of the slope giving access onto the lane to Walton Wood Lodge. Continue straight over via Burtholme Beck footbridge and stile; in a few yards go left through the kissing-gate in the Wall hedge. Notice evidence of the Wall core running up the hill for 33 yards beneath the hedge: the Turf Wall ran a few yards to the north. A further kissing-gate is succeeded briefly by more stone Wall core. Turret 54b stood hereabouts, originally built of clay in the Turf Wall: a practice still evidenced locally as 'clay-biggins', witness several cottages at Walton. When the stone Wall was constructed in the late 190s A.D., it was placed on top of the turret. Proceed to a kissing-gate, smartly succeeded by a stile, with the path ascending marshy pasture beside the merest trace of the Wall's line. Cross the stile onto the road near Garthside. A left turn would bring the walker back down to Lanercost.

However, despite the lack of Wall excitement ahead, a visit to Howgill Farm holds a certain merit: N.B. if you are not equipped to cope with mud, follow the road instead. Cross the road, pass through the gate, traverse an improved pasture containing the faintest hint of Wall ditch, to the gate. Descend with the hedge on the left, to sweep round the marshy, cattle poached, hollow, rising beyond to a frequently excessively muddy gate on the left. Turn immediately right via a gate into the farm lane.

Go left, pass the entrance to Howgill Farm, notice the two railway freight carriages, potentially of great historical interest to railway buffs. The Pathfinder map alludes to an inscribed Roman stone in the vicinity, a centurial stone commemorating the work on the Wall by 'civitas catuvellaunorum', the people from St.Albans (Verulamium): unfortunately it is not publicly visible though located in a modern wall.

Entering the pasture via a gate descend into the valley, keep left following the hedge to a gate onto the road. Stay on the road to Burtholme Farm ('burt' is the same as 'bird' in Birdoswald and simply meant 'shelter', the full name meaning 'shelter on the raised land in a valley'). At Burtholme Bridge, cross the stile to follow the footpath signposted 'Lanercost Bridge'; note the three trees beside the beck, their metal protector fences well and truly grown-in thus killing the trees they were intended to defend. A stile puts the footpath beside a hedgeline leading south-east away from Burtholme Beck. Just before the end of the field, go through the kissing-gate. Proceed beside the Irthing, an ancient river-name, probably meaning 'river stained with earth': admire the fine view ahead comprising the old and new Abbey Bridges. Complete the walk by crossing the wall-stile onto the old bridge, the exclusive province of pedestrian admiration. What a delight it is to stand within the break-water refuges and gaze into the river below - with the bonus of the Abbey Bridge Hotel for timely refreshment.

Short walk via LANERCOST PRIORY to the WALL

Parking at Lanercost Bridge, follow the footpath, signposted 'Island Cottages', beside the river to just before it parts company with the Irthing. Go left towards the Priory ruins via the gate into the paddock on the east side. Proceed beside the wall to a gate left, keep north of the Priory to the road exit at the ruined barbican arch. Turn right, then straight on at the junction between the cottages going up the bridle-lane. Where the lane forks, go right, ascending to a gate. Keep on the track to Haytongate. Turn left to accompany the Wall path down to the Walton Lodge track. Do not cross Burtholme Beck, instead go left upon the track skirting Abbey Gill Wood to regain Lanercost.

from TINDALE ______________________________________

4½ mile circular walk featuring:
Tarn House, Howgill and Tarnhouse Rigg

Tindale Tarn

The walk begins from the old mining hamlet of Tindale, situated 2½ miles east of Hallbankgate; perhaps it might be germane to mention the Belted Will Inn as a valuable refreshment back-stop. Tindale derives its name from its situation as an old entry point into the Tyne valley from the Gelt via Talkin. It emerged in recent centuries as a community of colliers, zinc smelters and lime-kiln operatives serviced by the Brampton/Lambley sub-branch railway.

START grid ref. NY 617593

Park on the open space beside the RSPB notice-board. Heed the map defining the reserve and associated rights-of-way network. Follow the track which winds down to a bridge over Tarn Beck and rises to the Pennine Trail Riding Centre. The clinker banks to the left being all that remains from a zinc spelter works. Quite the majority of the clinker having been removed and used as hardcore during the laying of the military road network on Spadeadam Waste in the 1950s, specifically for Blue Streak rocket testing, it's now used to train pilots, hence the frequency of low flying jets.

Pass the bungalow 'Bishophill' to a gate. The footpath proceeds as an open track passing a crumbling yet still imposing twin arched lime-kiln. Immediately after notice evidence of a tramway which diverged to the old Bishop Hill colliery, with a branch traversing the slopes of Bruthwaite to the Venture Drift mine above Howgill. Pass through a gateway with attendant tin sheds, admire the pictur-esque setting of Tindale Tarn ahead, before swinging left with the green track. This was the location of the 1995

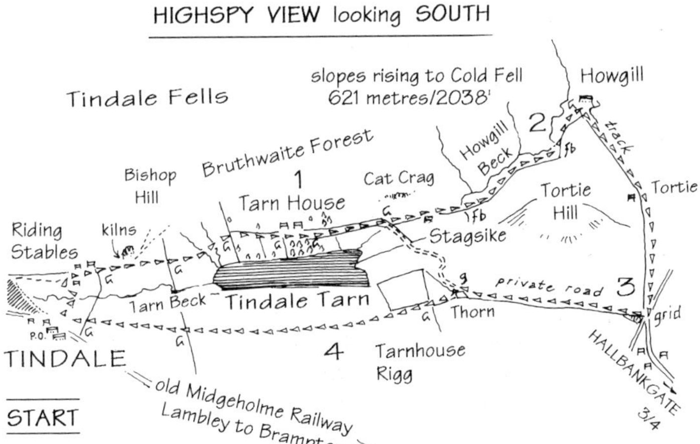

'One man and his Dog' television sheepdog trial series. At a gate the track enters the sycamore sheltered enclosures approaching Tarn House. In negotiating the yard gates the walker is unlikely to go unheeded by the resident collies. A very well disguised C15th peel tower lurks within the fabric of this fine old farmhouse, despite the comparatively recent date, 1813, inscribed above the porch. Proceeding down the access lane see right the remains of a sheep wash and beyond the reed beds at the head of the tarn. This RSPB preserve attracts a huge array of birdlife, year round, Whopper Swans being notable regular winter visitors. Where the access track bears right, go left through the gate on the signposted footpath passing beneath Cat Crags, a reference to the polecat, and Stagsike, a derelict dwelling originally housingtwo shepherds, ornamented with a coat of arms and the date 1883. Follow the wall via a footbridge, hereon accompanying Howgill Beck, crossing a rotting sleeper footbridge advancing to the hamlet of Howgill.

Up to the left rise mine scarred and terraced slopes and the wild valley head of Howgill Beck drawing attention towards the distant, convex slope obscured summit of Cold Fell. A windshelter built upon a huge tumulus cairn marks the focus of ascents. Aspiring peak-baggers are not at liberty to approach direct from Howgill, the inviting bulldozed track being for the exclusive use of shepherds and gamekeepers. The only sure line of ascent follows the fence over Brown Fell, reached via the bridleway accompanying the old Gairs Colliery track. Should you be tempted to make the climb please respect the fact that all this high ground is sensitively managed nature reserve and refrain from wandering at will. Hill-walkers will know this 2037/621m summit to be the 225th in order of altitude in England & Wales, that it is one foot lower than High Willhays, the highest point on Dartmoor and one foot higher than Snaefell, the highest point on the Isle of Man, and of course the northernmost point of the Pennine chain.

Pass through the gate before the row of cottages proceeding right leaving the environs of Howgill north via a galvanised gate and on down the road that forms the hamlet's link with the outside world. Pass the lone shuttered cottage Tortie a weekend home with a nicely tended garden. Crossing a cattle grid where the old mineral railway disected the road, go right across the cattle grid along the private road to Tarn House.

Crossing the brow a footpath is waymarked left passing below the lone crab apple tree at the twin sheepfold, named Thorn on OS maps, to reach a wicket-gate. Bear left then advance east keeping to the south side of the fence accompanying a bridleway to a gate. Continue with the fence now to the right, where this departs right, descending towards the reed bed at the head of Tindale Tarn. Continue on a discernible path through the rushy pasture passing a weathered boundary stone gradually declining from the upper part of Tarnhouse Rigg to a weighted hand-gate (wet environs) in a wall.

The first occasion I walked this way followed the laborious ascent of Cold Fell. By that stage in the day the cloud atmospherics were truly magical, spilling setting sun reddened vapour down the fellsides. The footpath leads on through the rushy pasture to regain the play area at Tindale via a gate. The large house in the middle, known as The Emporium, was the former Co-op shop; to the left Post Office Terrace contains an active post office: the sub-postmistress and her husband being the only true natives of Tindale, and proud too of a community which has exchanged the dirt and sweat of industry for that of an accessible retreat for artists and seekers after a less clamorous style of life.

The road from Howgill

from LOW GELT BRIDGE

4½ mile circular walk featuring:
The wooded gorge of lower Geltsdale.

Causewayed path in the gorge near the Written Rock of Gelt

START grid ref. NY 520592

Situated near the attractive market town of Brampton, Gelt Woods wins a special place in this selection of choice Wall Country walks. This is not merely because the Romans came here to extract sandstone to repair their military 'march', as evidenced by the 'Written Rock', etched by soldiers from the 2nd legion, but particularly because it makes such a satisfying walk, alive with an abundance of natural history interest. Leave the Low Gelt Bridge car park crossing

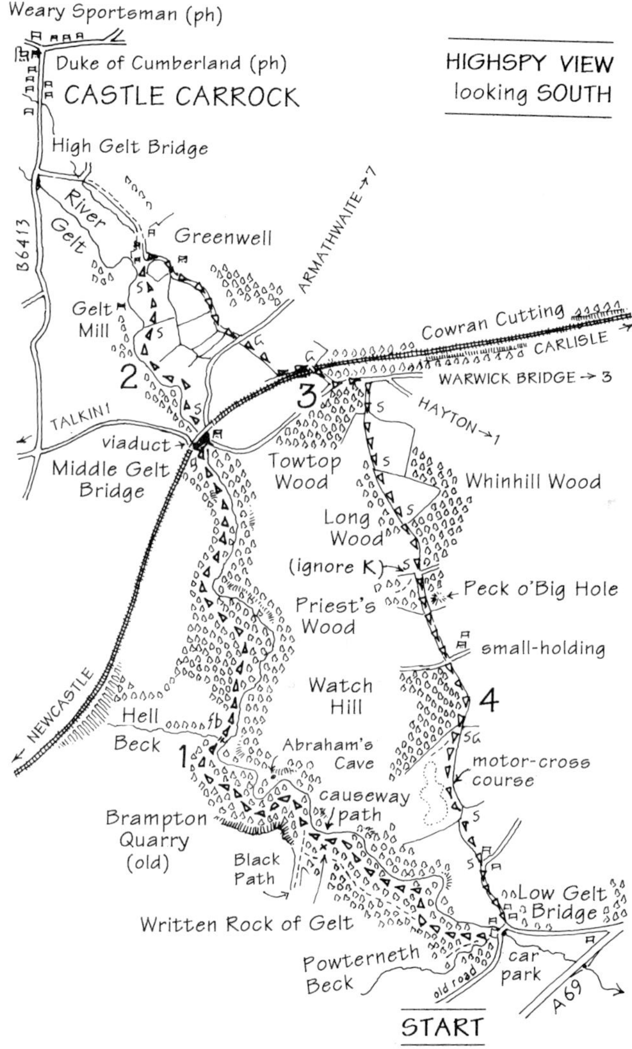

Weary Sportsman (ph)
Duke of Cumberland (ph)
CASTLE CARROCK
High Gelt Bridge
B6413
River Gelt
Greenwell
ARMATHWAITE → 7
Gelt Mill
HIGHSPY VIEW
looking SOUTH
Cowran Cutting
CARLISLE
WARWICK BRIDGE → 3
HAYTON → 1
TALKIN 1
2
3
viaduct
Middle Gelt Bridge
Towtop Wood
Whinhill Wood
Long Wood
(ignore K)
Peck o' Big Hole
Priest's Wood
small-holding
Watch Hill
4
NEWCASTLE
Hell Beck
fb
1
Abraham's Cave
motor-cross course
Brampton Quarry (old)
causeway path
Black Path
Low Gelt Bridge
Written Rock of Gelt
Powterneth Beck
old road
car park
A69
START

Powterneth Beck. 'Pow' means 'slow moving', while 'terneth' comes from the British 'tern' meaning 'torrent', which is descriptive of its final fling into the Gelt.

Owned by Brampton Town Council, Low Gelt Woods are sensitively managed by the Royal Society for the Protection of Birds (RSPB). Please respect their endeavours to hold a diverse, and minimally disturbed, habitat. After the initial rise the path reaches a seat, then forks. The upper path can be used as a useful means of return for visitors wishing to take only a short stroll, perhaps back-tracking from Hellbeck footbridge. The main path leads down the right-hand path which slants towards the river. An early detour from the path to the river's tight bend dramatically illustrates the origin of the name 'Gelt' deriving from the Scandinavian settlers' term meaning 'mad water'. Follow the river upstream along a causewayed path consolidated in 1968 in place of a cantilevered footway. The enticing steps clambering up the outcrop over-bearing the river was the way to the Written Rock of Gelt: not only are the steps perilous, but the etchings are no longer decipherable, so don't risk it. Alfred Lord Tennyson in his 'Idylls of the King' made an apt reference to the inscription as 'crag-carven o'er the streaming Gelt'.

The path gradually rises to join the Black Path from Brampton, which served as a direct route to the old Brampton Quarries which dominate the path as it winds upstream. The source of much of the town's building stone this vertical wall reaches a height of 140 feet and is patterned with a distinctive scoring from the action of quarrymen's picks. This quarry supplied the stone for St. Martin's Church, Brampton. Built in 1878, St. Martin's is unique in being the only church designed by the pre-Raphaelite architect Philip Webb; his work elsewhere is notable in its diversity.

Well screened though it may be by summer growth Abraham's Cave lurks amongst the crags on the west side of the valley, created in 1814 by a gamekeeper, presumably as a hideout to assist in the detection and apprehension of poachers.

The path descends to cross the Hellbeck footbridge. From hereon Middle Gelt Wood is characterised by its predominance of conifers, progressively being thinned by the RSPB to encourage oak regeneration. **Reach Middle Gelt Bridge via a wicket gate.** The huge skew viaduct completed in 1835 soars overhead. You may notice that the architect's and builder's epithets are displayed on the arches in both Latin and English.

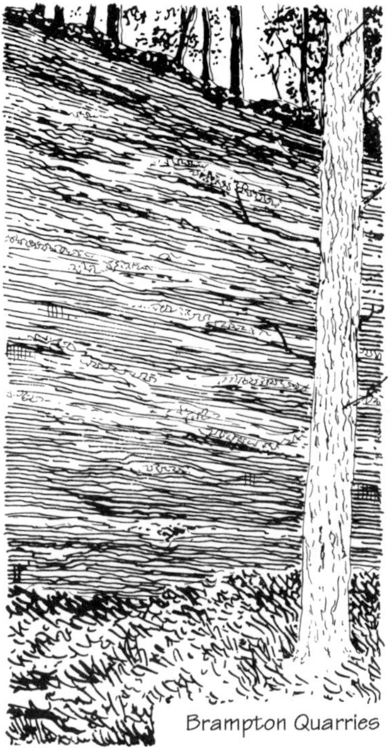

Brampton Quarries

Cross the road bridge, built in 1723, pass the former coaching inn, known as the Graham's Arms. Though closed in the early 1970s, it is still shown as a public house on current Pathfinder maps. **Follow the road under the viaduct, after 70 yards cross the stile left following the river through meadows. Cross a series of stiles to reach the road in the hamlet of Greenwell.**

Should you wish to make a lunchtime rendezvous with a refreshing 'pint and ploughmans' continue south through the hamlet, along the bridle-track and lane to the B6413 at High Gelt Bridge. It is just 800 yards to Castle Carrock village and a choice of two good pubs.

Greenwell

The walk continues by bearing sharp right south along the winding road. Go straight across at the junction through the facing gate. The bridle-way follows the hedge to the railway fence bearing left to the brick bridge over Cowran Cutting. When the Newcastle to Carlisle Railway was constructed in the early 1830s the Gelt formed a formidable obstacle. Both the viaduct and the mile long cutting represented major engineering triumphs of their age. The rather odd name Cowran could have its roots in Thief Street along the route traced to Low Gelt Bridge: for this was the route frequently taken by cattle rustlers

Cowran Cutting

from over the border. This also explains 'Watch Hill' where Hayton people will have lain in wait to challenge raiders.

Joining the road look east across the valley towards the village of Talkin, backed by Cold Fell and the King's Forest of Geltsdale. Go left, then right beside Towtop Woods, follow the lane to a stile, keep beside the hedge north-north-west. Cross two more stiles, enter a fenced passage beside Whinhill Wood, and at the next stile proceed along a lane passing Peck o'Big Hole, a wooded hollow where cattle thieves may well have held out till the way was clear.

At the cross-tracks the bridle-lane continues north. After the stile/gate the path enters the Hollow Bank motor-cross course. Keeping close to the lefthand fence, descend the sandy track graced with abundant gorse and broom, to a stile. Continue beside the fence to a small dutch barn and stile onto the road. The sleepy barn down the road is the hideout of barn owls; don't disturb!

from NEWTOWN ___________________________________

3 mile circular walk featuring:
The course of Hadrian's Wall and Irthington

St. Kentigern's, Irthington

Newtown is situated on the A6071 2 miles west of Brampton. This hamlet, within the Irthington parish, was a 'new township' in late Saxon times! The settlement originally established on the route from Brampton into Scotland via Longtown, has more recently attracted commuters from Carlisle, complete with 'dormitory-style' housing.

START grid ref. NY 500628

The walk begins from the open ground/sports field.

Follow the Irthington road south-west on line with Hadrian's Wall, pass the unmarked location of Milecastle

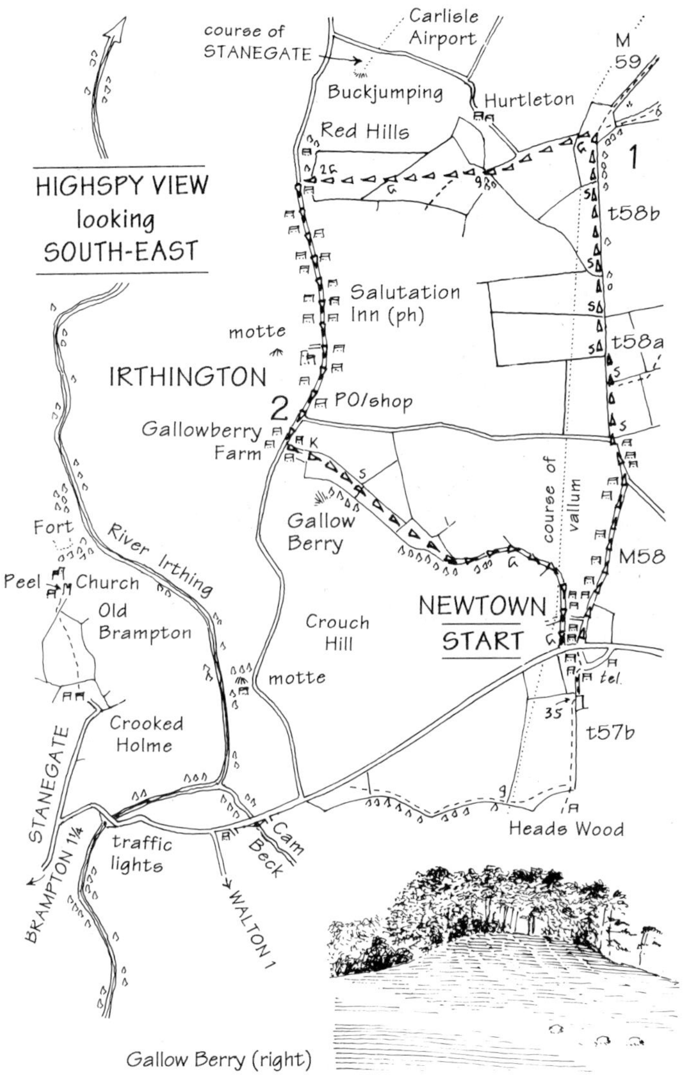

Gallow Berry (right)

58. Leave the road beyond the junction, where it bears sharp left, go right to a stile/footpath sign next to 'Westwinds'. Both footpath and hedgeline continue along the line of Hadrian's Wall, with only the faint north ditch confirming this fact. The ditch becomes more evident following the next stile, beyond which switch sides of the hedge via a simple, waymarked, stile at the site of turret 58a. Turret 58b and three

Remnant north ditch of Hadrian's Wall

stiles further the ditch line curves right, giving an attractive glimpse down the original Leofhere's valley from which the parish-name 'Laversdale' derived.

Reaching the lane gate, turn obliquely left upon the bridle-way across the pasture to a waymarked gate. Crossing the line of the ploughed out vallum, follow the righthand hedge through a fenced passage then descend the hollow-way to a hunting-gate. Within this scarp the soil is remarkably powdery when dry, and its tree shaded banks are popular with cattle and sheep, not to mention foxes.

The bridle-way strikes directly down the pasture, keeping to the foot of the righthand slope. Pass through the gate in the new wire fence to enter the village street in Irthington via two gates and a private drive. Follow the street north past the Salutation Inn, the Post Office/village shop and parish church. Just beyond the road junction, next to Gallowberry Farm, the sign-posted footpath branches left. Pass through the kissing-gate. Notice the pine shrouded knoll of Gallowberry ahead, the name confirming that an intimidating gibbet once stood there as a portent to any potential miscreants. Ascend to the lefthand fence to a stile, follow the clear path beneath the bracken slope into the shy valley. Continue along an attractive lane, via a gate, latterly swinging right in sympathy with the vallum, past the florally lovely Lilac Cottage, to emerge, via a side stepped gate, on the A6071 at Newtown.

Salutation Inn, Irthington

from LAVERSDALE

6½ mile circular walk featuring:
The course of Hadrian's Wall and Scaleby Castle

Southern aspect of Scaleby Castle

START grid ref. NY 476626

Approach Laversdale (meaning 'Leofhere's valley') from the Brampton/Longtown A6071 road, either via Laversdale Lane or via Irthington passing the eastern end of Carlisle Airport. This quiet hamlet, within the Irthington parish, is by-passed by all main roads just north of Hadrian's Wall.

From opposite The Sportsman, serving the locally brewed Theakston beers, follow the side road east passing the village school, via the white washed housing to a bridle-way sign/gate. Entering pastureland advance to a gate/bridleway waymark, keeping the hedge to your left. Angle half right to a kissing-gate. Keeping right follow the valley hedge to a further gate/bridleway waymark into a seldom trod bridle-lane (though not overgrown). At the next gate/bridleway waymark the lane broadens with light woodland. Proceed to yet another gate/bridle-

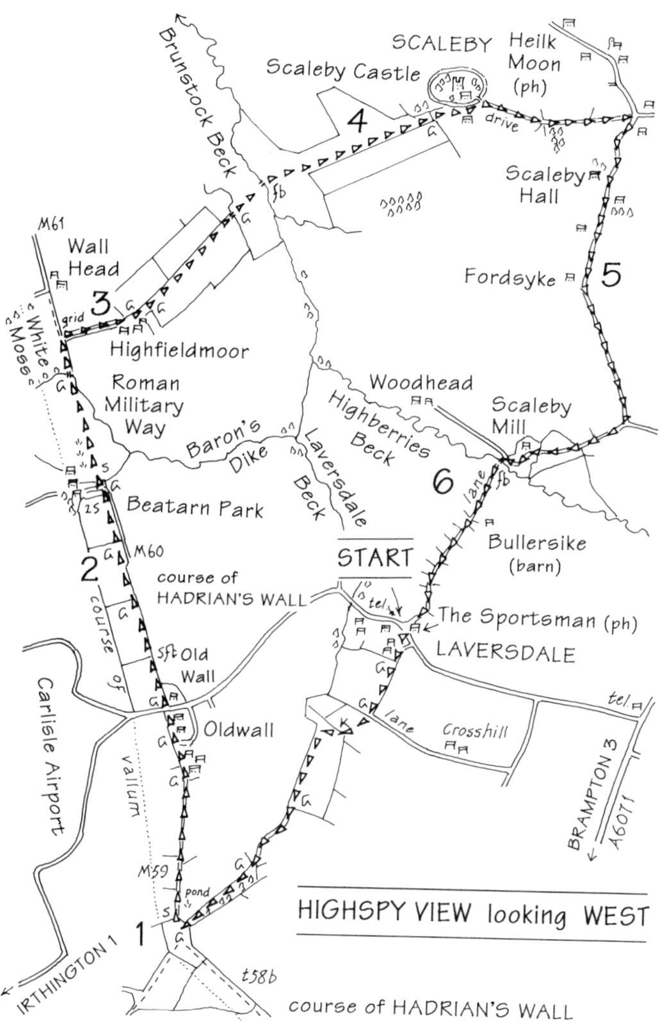

Brunstock Beck
SCALEBY
Scaleby Castle
Heilk Moon (ph)
4
drive
Scaleby Hall
M61
Wall Head
3
grid
White Moss
Highfieldmoor
Roman Military Way
Fordsyke
5
Baron's Dike
Laversdale Beck
Woodhead
Highberries Beck
Scaleby Mill
6
lane
fb
Beatarn Park
25
G
M60
2
course of HADRIAN'S WALL
START
tel
Bullersike (barn)
The Sportsman (ph)
LAVERSDALE
Carlisle Airport
vallium
Sft Old Wall
G
Oldwall
lane
Crosshill
tel
BRAMPTON 3
A6071
M59
pond
S
G
1
t58b
IRTHINGTON 1
HIGHSPY VIEW looking WEST
course of HADRIAN'S WALL

way waymark. Turn right on the line of Hadrian's Wall to the fence stile/footpath waymark, enter the green lane running on the course of the Roman turf and stone embankment, passing without trace the site of Milecastle 59. At Old Wall Farm, a handsome vernacular farmhouse with well-tended garden, a gate heralds the end of the lane. After new and old farm buildings the open lane proceeds through a gate along the access road, passes three houses to reach the minor road. You can curtail the outing, right, to reach Laversdale, making a walk of 2¾ miles. However, there is clear evidence of the Wall ditch next to the course of the Wall, which would be a pity to miss by shortening the walk at this point. Cross the Laversdale road via the gate (footpath sign), advance with the hedge on your right, through the pasture to a stile/footbridge. Continuing, beyond the next gate a kink in the hedgeline gives a view of the bank looking back. To the right, a green lane separated by the fenced off ditch runs parallel with the footpath. The site of Milecastle 60 is situated just prior to the next gate in a modern fence. Note the bulrushes in the ditch, forerunners of many in the overgrown lake at Bleatarn. It is rather odd that the footpath does not run within the lane. Approaching Bleatarn Farm the footpath passes through a paddock via two stiles, descends into, and crosses the lane to a gate and small square enclosure before continuing to a frail stile. To the left, resting upon

Bleatarn Park from the Roman Military Way

the vallum, is the buttressed Bleatarn Park. The path proceeds along the pasture ridge, beside Blea Tarn beset with rushes and reeds, the eroded Wall ditch evident to the right. The bank, a shallow causeway, is a surviving portion of the Roman Military Way. Cross at the gate Baron's Dike, draining White Moss. With the track advancing towards the road at Wall Head turn right into the farm lane, signposted bridleway to Scaleby, immediately after the new concrete farm access road. Proceed straight through Highfieldmoor Farm, passing the farmhouse via gates. *You might as well forget the tempting bridleway short-cut leading right from the metal gate and along a concrete track bound for Laversdale as this has been barbed wired off in several places very securely.*

All Saints, Scaleby

The bridle-way to Scaleby runs through pastures grazed by beef cattle. Its course initially runs with the hedge on the left. Continue to the gated bridge over the slow moving Brunstock Beck, draining the flat basin below Laversdale. From the bridge the bridle-way angles from north-west to north-north-west through very poor rushy pasture (there is a hedgeline after 200 yards) leading to a gate and passes the east side of Scaleby Castle moat. Scaleby Castle is the home of Lord Henley, a prominent Peer and former chairman of the CPRE, related to the Earl of Carlisle of Naworth Castle. The parish church has memorials to his Victorian predecessors the Fawcetts and Farrers. Scaleby dates from the fourteenth century and it is pleasing to see a moat still functioning, serving to enhance the castle's gorgeously maintained gardens and grounds rather than repel aggressive visitations! Despite the lack of public access, the castle is clearly viewed from the bridle-way as it passes on through the adjoining farmyard to reach the castle drive. Going right, exit onto the village street at the 'T' junction: beyond All Saints Church, 800 yards to the left, is The Heilk Moon public house. Should you have set your store on The Sportsman being open on your return then hasten right directly from the junction. Follow the road for a little under a mile to the road branching right bound for Scaleby Mill and Woodhead Farm. Watch for the left turn over Highberries Beck as the road sweeps right after Scaleby Mill, major refurbishment complete with stabling. Crossing the footbridge enter a delightful green lane.

Highberries Beck and the lane by Bullersike

The Sportsman, Laversdale

The Heilk Moon, Scaleby

from BEAUMONT

4½ mile circular walk featuring:
The River Eden and the course of Hadrian's Wall

River Eden from Kirkandrews, with Cold Fell forming a distant backdrop

START grid ref. NY 349593

This walk starts at Beaumont, pronounced 'Beemunt', situated on a low ridge three miles west of Carlisle, overlooking the tidal Eden. St.Mary's Church was built on a mound where once stood part of Hadrian's Wall and turret 70a: residual Roman masonry was inevitably incorporated in the church fabric. Begin from the green at the heart of this charming agricultural community, which lives up to its name 'beautiful hill'.

Follow the lane leading east for 200 yards thus joining the Cumbria Coastal Way via the wicket-gate on the right. This stretch of path, constantly being undermined by the tidal Eden, has been strengthened with retaining planks and hand-rails as the footpath traverses through the steep wooded bank. Descending to a footbridge over Monkhill Beck, the path mounts the opposite bank joining the 'hypothesised' course of Hadrian's Wall - times like this test one's imagination!

Keeping close to the fence, advance via two stiles to a three way footpath sign (viewpoint for drawing at the head of this walk). Descending the bank, follow the riverbank: just prior to crossing the Doudle Beck footbridge I delighted in watching both a great crested grebe and a heron fishing. This, the Carhead Stream of the Eden, is a popular stretch with fishermen, feathered and oil-skinned alike, the soft-footed species 'walker vulgaris' only rarely causing disturbance.

A stile leads the riverside path to the start of a lane. Pass through the gate left, ignore Cherrim Lane as it breaks right direct to Grinsdale, keep to the river bank meadow. Just visible a ¼ mile distant, across the river, stands the village of Cargo, a curious name thought to be a hybrid from the Welsh *carreg* 'rock' and Nordic *haugr* 'hill'. The path negotiates three fence stiles. Notice a cave in the far bank beneath the wooded cliff; the hill is crowned with the oval earthworks of an Iron Age settlement. The Eden, known at this point as the Coop Stream, curves tightly round to the south.

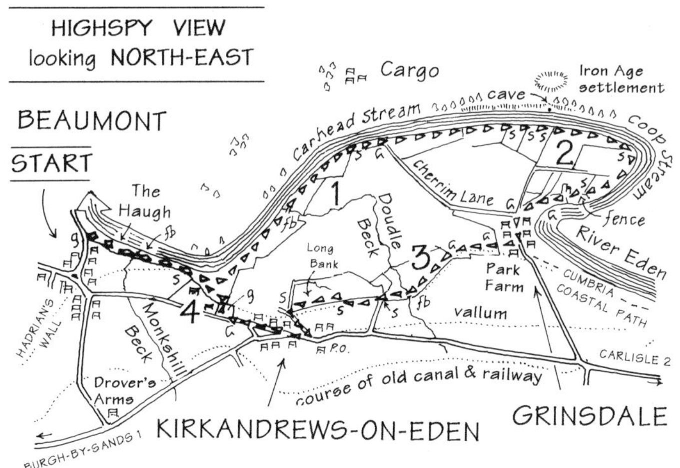

Cave beneath the Iron Age fort on the Cargo shore of the Eden

The spring on the far bank, at the bend of the river, was once considered to have healing properties, hence Spa Well (sulphureous). Looking south Carrock Fell, High Pike and Skiddaw are in view. The riverside path approaches Grinsdale's small pebble-dashed church, via a stile, then fence. Turn right to enter the churchyard. Though the church is kept locked its charming exterior and setting are a pleasure to behold: note the arms of George III on the west wall. Follow the church access via gates into Coophouse Lane and Grinsdale village street.

Turn right through the gated farmyard of Park Farm, footpath sign 'Beaumont': note the old brick setts still evident in the cattle yards. A track proceeding through pasture rises upon a bank to join, imperceptibly, the course of Hadrian's Wall. Go through the gate, follow the hedge down to Sourmilk Bridge; one would have thought it rare for Doudle Beck, known as Hopsteps Beck higher upstream, to resound in bubbling spate like milk. Follow the hedge, with sprigs of gorse on line with the Wall, to the inviting entrance to a lane. Cross the stile in the fence to the right. Proceed along the Wall's course with the double fence to your right. Cross the stile to a path along the top of a steep bank: the route is confirmed by the stile in the short fence linking to a trio of cherry trees. Descending the bank via the stile enter the green lane, turn left to enter Kirkandrews. Kirkandrews-on-Eden, though still possessing a church-yard, lost its 'kirk' dedicated to the Celtic saint in 1692 when the parish merged Beaumont. Go right, along the village street, taking the righthand fork by the cottage with millstone. 120 yards after the junction follow the Beaumont footpath sign via a gate right. Go left to the wicket-gate, then right, round the old grass tennis courts belonging to Beaumont Parish Sports Club. Continue along the bank to the three-way footpath sign. Here rejoin the outward route.

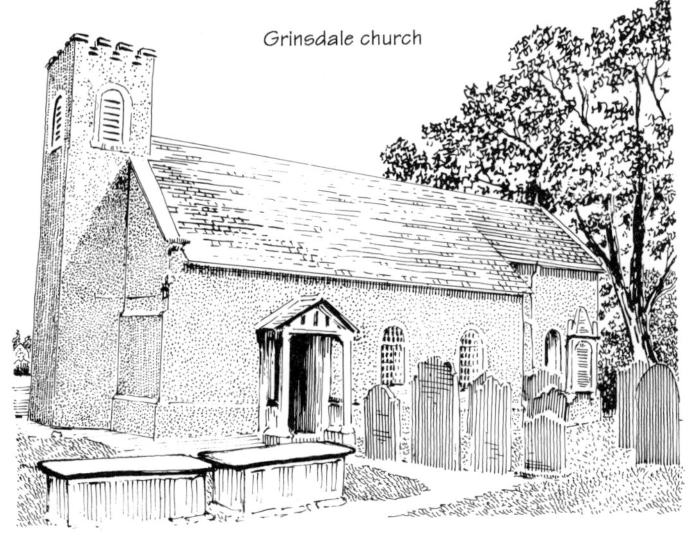

Grinsdale church

from PORT CARLISLE

3 mile circular walk featuring:
Bowness-on-Solway and Port Carlisle

Canal basin at Port Carlisle

START grid ref. NY 242619

Park on the broad verge beside the Solway Methodist Chapel, beautifully refurbished and decorated in 1992. Follow the green lane leading south via a gate. After 250 yards cross the course of the vallum at the site of turret 78a, detectable in the pasture over to the left. Reaching a gate at the end of the lane, bear right following the hedge, keep within the field, round the corner, gently ascend to a gate entering a second green lane. Advance to Brackenrigg Farm passing through two gates by the sheep pen, turn right along

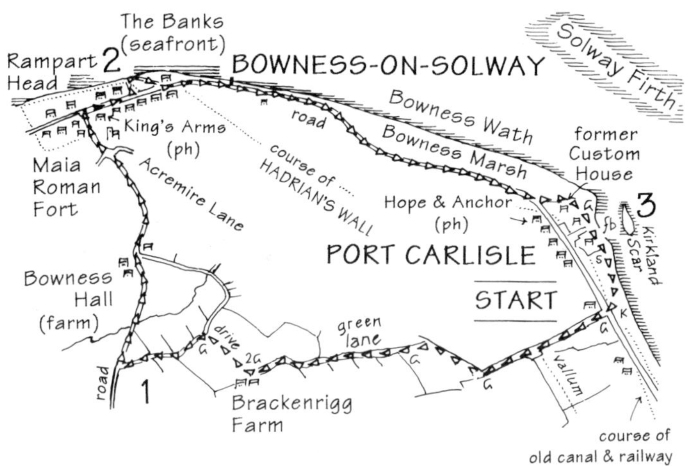

HIGHSPY VIEW looking NORTH

the concrete farm access drive. At the farm gate, go left within the farm lane to join the minor road. Go right passing Bowness Hall Farm to enter Bowness. Note the, now rare, 'cats-eyed' village sign.

The parish church of St.Michael standing on a mound, just outside the boundary of Maia Roman Fort, merits a visit. The church, a sturdy buttressed sandstone structure smothered in pale lichen, inevitably features Wall-stone, most notably in the west end beneath the bell-cote and to the east of the window by the pulpit.

On reaching the road junction beside the King's Arms note the wall plaque detailing the plan of Maia. Go right for 140 yards to enter the passage signposted 'The Banks', on the eastern edge of the Roman fort. This brief parade to the Rampart Head shore represents Bowness' sea-front with a broad view across the Solway to Chapel-cross Power Station and Annan, and westward to Criffel and the Colvend Coast with the old lighthouse on Souther-ness Point, which stands near the birthplace of John Paul Jones, accredited as the founder of the United States Navy.

Follow the pathway round, and back into the narrow village street. Head out of the village along the road, though after Grey Havens, set upon a bank against possible flood, it is practical to walk along the edge of Bowness Marsh to Port Carlisle. Branch left proceeding on the track past the old Custom House, to a gate and bridge crossing the mouth of the old canal, formerly Carlisle's commercial link with the larger vessels on the open waters of the Solway.

Continue on round, via the stile onto the saltings thus returning to the point of departure some 300 yards south of the canal crossing.

Catamaran beached on the Bowness Wath shore

BACK TO THE WALL

For the last eight years it has been my undoubted pleasure to journey from time to time back to the Wall. My first mission to devise a route more or less from coast to coast, from Segedunum to Maia - Volume One The WALL WALK was the result. And now my varied wanderings have resulted in this collection of circular walks, exploring the breadth of the region.

The excessive period indulged in creating these two modest books reflects most of all a growing personal pleasure in this historic region. There is a discernible vibrance within the Solway/Tyne arena. Having visited numerous pubs by day and night, I have stirring memories of listening to *Savage Amusement's* rendition of "The North Shall Rise". From the Tyne Gap to either hand rise the Pennines and the dark serried ranks of the Border Forest, to the east the Whin Sill and westward the Solway Firth as a silver sheet.

Like any borderland worth its salt it lies more at the heart of matters than at the fringe; as any cursory study of a map of Britain will show, there is an undeniable centrality. It's no wonder that Haltwhistle has seized the initiative to market itself as the 'Centre of Britain'. What this seeks to illuminate is that Hadrian's Wall is but one ingredient in a beautifully diverse landscape, a rich tapestry of the affairs of man and nature.

Hadrian's Wall holds a special appeal as an objective for the walker with history in their veins. William Hutton set the pace back in 1802 when he walked from Birmingham to the Wall and back at the ripe old age of 78. Such feats of inquisitive endurance are an inspiration. Even as I write George Riley of Stoke-on-Trent, a more than sprightly octogenarian, is embarking upon a sponsored march along the Wall from Heddon to Bowness in support of the Douglas Macmillan Hospice, and I'm delighted that he is using my WALL WALK guide as his trusty companion. I am sure he will not be disappointed; my experience of the Wall is as much of the people who live and work there, as of the landscape itself. There is a genuine warmth in the rural community that he, and any visitor who is prepared to make an extended pedestrian stay, will quickly sense.

The ease with which the tourist can skip from site to site by car has made too many think of it as a whistle-stop destination. If you are visiting the Wall put it in mind to devote at least a full week to the experience and do it all on foot - best of luck George!

HADRIAN'S WALL PATH National Trail

The early work of this project was begun by Andrew Coleman. His successor, David McGlade, is carrying it through formal consultation towards inauguration. It is no simple task; to implant a formal pedestrian walkway upon an historic monument is a tricky business. Dave comes from the Offa's Dyke Path scene and knows from that a level of the concerns that potentially could form a conflicting buffer to such worthy plans. Hence his work concentrates on allaying fears towards the alignment of a sensitively prepared, largely greensward, walk. He is taking into consideration the necessary long-term con-cerns and wishes of landowners, farmers and archaeolo-gists; for the walker to feel at ease and know the real thrill of the experience they must know they are not intruding or inflicting any permanent injury on the monument. Only when it is fully complete in every detail will the distinctive acorn waymark appear. Before such time only footpath signs will guide the new generation of Wall-walkers. It is hoped that the trail will be up and ready, with fanfares for the year 2001 - speed the day.